E

The Potter' s P

Some passages (especially Romans 9) appear to support Calvinism, but does God really predestine particular persons for heaven or hell? And where is the knowledgeable expositor who also possesses an irenic disposition to answer such critical questions? Leighton Flowers nobly meets these qualifications and approaches the Scripture with a passion for the original language and context. We are all deeply in his debt for teaching us to hear God's Word so much better than we did before this book was written. Highly recommended.

– **Dr. Malcolm B. Yarnell III,**
Research Professor of Systematic Theology,
Author of *God the Trinity: Biblical Portraits and*
Royal Priesthood in the English Reformation and
The Formation of Christian Doctrine

The Potter's Promise *is the fascinating pilgrimage of Leighton Flowers, Director of Apologetics and Youth Evangelism for Texas Baptists. Chronicled here is his journey out of Calvinism and into a New Testament faith through the saving grace of our Lord. This may well be the most important volume published this year for the reading of every young servant of Christ. Do you have the courage to read it?*

– **Dr. Paige Patterson,**
President of Southwestern
Baptist Theological Seminary

In The Potter's Promise, *Dr. Leighton Flowers reveals, by means of a refreshingly clear and persuasive writing style, the theological and philosophical arguments that compelled him to abandon his previously Calvinistic convictions. While some Traditionalists have a tendency to avoid certain Bible verses, Dr. Flowers tackles them fear-lessly, placing them in their proper context in a manner consistent with the entirety of God's Word. Calvinists have sometimes been known to object to Traditional writers and thinkers by making the claim, "You just don't understand Calvinism." Any such charge leveled against Dr. Flowers rings hollow. Having heard all the arguments Calvinism has to offer, he nevertheless disaffirms it. Every Calvinist needs to read this book to challenge their thinking and con-sider the other side. Every Traditionalist needs to read this book to become better equipped in defending their own view of salvation doctrine.*

– Dr. Rick Patrick,
Executive Director of Connect 316 and
Senior Pastor

Confused by the issues surrounding Calvinism? Does Romans 9 teach unconditional predestination? Want to cut through some of the red tape? Then read Leighton's book. He is charitable but gets right to the point, making a strong, biblical case for a God who is glorified by sacrific-ing Himself for creation and not by sacrificing creation for Himself. He makes a strong case for the God of Jesus Christ.

– Austin Fischer,
Pastor and Author of *Young,*
Restless, No Longer Reformed.

Dr. Flowers' masterful treatment of the biblical text, and his philosophically consistent reasoning, is sure to sat-isfy the pallet of the academically interested. Yet, his acces-sible writing leads to a rare accomplishment. Lay readers will have no difficulty understanding the Calvinist posi-tions and the best responses to them. Any related bibliog-raphy that does not include Dr. Flowers masterful work will, henceforth, surely look odd.

– Dr. Braxton Hunter,
President of Trinity College
of the Bible and Theological Seminary

The Potter's Promise

A Biblical Defense of
Traditional Soteriology

By Leighton C. Flowers, D.Min

Director of Apologetics and
Youth Evangelism for Texas Baptists

The Bible quotations contained in this book are
from the New American Standard Bible, © by the
Lockman Foundation 1960, 1962, 1963, 1968, 1972,
1973, 1975, 1977; or The Holy Bible, New Interna-
tional Version ®, NIV ® Copyright © 1973, 1978,
1984, 2011 by Biblica, Inc.™ Used by permission. All
rights reserved.

ISBN-10:0-692-56184-6
ISBN-13:978-0-692-56184-3

CONTENTS

Introduction

From Calvinism to Traditionalism

As a Pastor and Professor of Theology who once affirmed Calvinism, I have a unique perspective on the biblical doctrine of salvation. However, I do not begrudge those who disagree with my views. I simply desire to correctly interpret the Word of God in order to understand Him rightly. Hopefully this book can help you understand why I could not continue to support the Calvinistic interpretation of the Scripture.

Since my journey out of Calvinism, many have expressed much interest in what specifics led me to recant my once beloved views. I suspect they are hoping to convince someone they care about to leave behind their Calvinistic beliefs. I hate to tell them, but it is doubtful that my story will accomplish that feat.

It is very difficult to convince oneself to leave a long held theological perspective and next to impossible to convince another. For me it was a painstaking three-year journey after I engaged in an in-depth study of the subject. I had no desire to leave Calvinism, and I fought tooth and nail to defend my beloved "doctrines of grace" against the truths my studies led me to see. There was no single argument, article, or discussion that led me to recant my adherence to the TULIP systematic.

In fact, I am quite certain I could never have been "debated out of Calvinism." I was much too competitive to objectively evaluate my systematic in the heat of a contentious type of discussion. Even if I were to come up against an argument I could not answer, I would have never admitted that to my opponent. Few individuals would be able to get around the intense emotion and pride inducing adrenaline brought on by debating theology. Our innate desire to be esteemed by others and seen as "smarter" than we really are often overwhelms any potential for learning and profitable dialogue.

If someone disagreed with me, my presumption was that they must not really understand my perspective. So, instead of attempting to listen and objectively evaluate their arguments, I focused on restating my case more clearly, confidently and dogmatically. If I did not fully understand what they were saying, I would often label and dismiss them instead of taking the time to fully evaluate their point of view. I am not attempting to suggest every Calvinist makes these errors - I am only reflecting on what I now view as my mistakes.

I competed on the state level in cross examination debate in high school and college. Our debate coach drilled into us the skill of taking on both the affirmative and negative side of every issue. And believe me, that is a learned skill. It is very difficult to put down one view in the defense of another opposing view, especially if you are emotionally and intellectually attached to a given perspective.

It is rare to find real objectivity in a discussion among theologically minded individuals over a doctrine as emotionally charged and intimately personal as that of our salvation. This is especially true of those who have made a living and developed their identity around a particular set of beliefs. Imagine R. C. Sproul, for example, coming to believe he was mistaken on these points of doctrine. Think how much it would cost him and his reputation as a scholar to recant his long held views. This is never an easy or painless transition for anyone at any level of notoriety.

I say all this to tell any Calvinistic readers who may have picked up this book in order to refute my claims: I am not so naive as to think my words are going to convince you to leave Calvinism, thus that is not my goal. My goal however, is that you simply understand the reasons I left Calvinism...and I mean *really* understand. That most likely cannot happen if you begin with an axe to grind or a point to defend. Can we put down the weapons and first seek to hear and fully understand each other before launching into a debate? If you finish this book and walk away still as Calvinistic as you are right now, but you fully understand why I felt I had to leave Calvinism, then I will consider this a great success.

Questioning Calvinism

I adopted all five points of the Calvinistic TULIP when I was a freshman in college after digesting books from John MacArthur, R.C. Sproul, J.I. Packer and later John Piper. Louie Giglio, the man who brought John Piper into the mainstream through events like Passion, is one of my father's friends. My first ministry position was with GRACE at Hardin-Simmons University, modeled after Louie's ministry at Baylor University in the '80s. Here is where I worked alongside Matt Chandler, having been mentored by the same pastor. I grew very convinced of Calvinism over the next decade of life, even helping to start a new Reformed Baptist Church that split off from my home church.

Later I served on staff at the new Reformed Church and then began working for the Texas Baptist state convention. We hired John Piper along with various other notable Calvinistic communicators to speak at many of the events I directed. I very much loved being a part of this "brotherhood" of ministers who proudly affirmed the doctrine of Spurgeon and the forefathers of our Southern Baptist faith. I was a card-carrying member of *The Founders* of the SBC and would never have dreamed that one day I would be writing these words.

One morning I was reading a book by A.W. Tozer, a man I knew was respected in the Calvinistic community. John Piper often quoted him and people referenced his works regularly in my Reformed circles. Some of what he wrote simply did not fit into my paradigm. As I read, I remember thinking to myself, "Isn't Tozer a Calvinist?" I distinctly remember how I felt when I learned that A.W. Tozer and later C.S. Lewis, two men I greatly respected, did not affirm the Calvinistic systematic. At that point, I recalled what my debate training taught me, and I realized I had never objectively and thoroughly vetted the scholarly views that oppose Calvinism. This started my journey.

Six months to a year into this study of soteriology, I was not the least bit convinced that Calvinism was wrong. Even after being presented with several convincing arguments against my long held beliefs, I subconsciously felt I had too much to lose to leave Calvinism. My reputation, my friends, my ministry connections - all gone if I recant my views on this! I had converted way too many people and hurt way too many relationships in defense of these views for me to go back on what I was so certain to be true for so many years. However, my years of training in debate helped me to recognize this bias and proceed with my studies nonetheless.

As I was trained, I forced myself to drop my preconceived ideas, my biases, and anything that might hinder me from fully understanding the other perspective. I wanted to know what godly, intelligent men like Tozer and Lewis saw in the Scriptures that led them to their conclusions. I wanted to fully vet their perspectives on soteriology.

In that process there were many key truths that came to light that eventually led me away from Calvinism. Elsewhere I write in more detail about all the points of doctrine with which I struggled,[1] but in this volume I wish to focus on the main biblical truths that came to light in my journey. My goal is to help the reader understand the non-Calvinistic interpretation of the Scriptures as well as some of the foundation arguments used to support the overall Calvinistic worldview.

In All Fairness

If you do not already know what Calvinism is all about, I recommend that you study the teachings of Calvinists themselves and keep in mind that not all Calvinists are the same.[2] Learn from my mistake; you should always study the opposition's viewpoint for yourself.

Back when I was a Calvinist, I had so saturated myself with Calvinistic preachers and authors that the only thing I knew of the opposing views was what they told me. Thus, I had been led to believe the only real alternative to Calvinism was this strange concept of

---

[1] See the author's blog and podcast at www.soteriology101.com

[2] Examples of other points where Calvinists simply do not agree among themselves: (1) Atonement: Phil Johnson, President of Grace to You ministries, writes, "But second, don't imagine that there is just one view for the Limited Atonement position and another view for the Unlimited Atonement position. As if there are two polar opposites here and they compete against each other. This is not really an either/or position even among Calvinists. And in fact, historically, the most intense debates about Limited Atonement have come over the past 400 years, they've all been intramural debates between Calvinists, among Calvinists... There are at least six possible Calvinists' interpretations of it [Scripture]..." Phil Johnson, *The Nature of the Atonement: Why and for Whom did Christ die?* Quote taken from: http://www.bible-bb.com/files/MAC/SC03-1027.htm; [date accessed: 4/2/15].. (2) God's Love for All, see John MacArthur, *Does God Love the World?* (3) Lapsarian Controversy (4) God's genuine desire for all to be saved (5) The "order salutis" (the temporal vs. logical order).

God "looking through the corridors of time to elect those He foresees would choose Him." Notable Calvinistic teachers almost always paint non-Calvinistic scholars as holding to this perspective. Once I realized I had been misled on this point, I was more open to consider other interpretations objectively. So, just as it is only fair to learn Calvinism from actual Calvinists, it is also only fair to learn Traditionalism from a Southern Baptist Traditionalist.[3]

With this in mind, here is a direct quote from John Calvin which most clearly reveals the Traditionalist's major point of contention with our Calvinistic brethren:

> "By predestination we mean the eternal decree of God, by which He determined with Himself whatever He wished to happen with regard to every man. All are not created on equal terms, but some are preordained to eternal life, others to eternal damnation; and, accordingly, as each has been created for one or other of those ends, we say that he has been predestined to life or death...[4] Some are predestined to salvation, others to damnation... Regarding the lost: it was His good pleasure to doom to destruction... Since the disposition of all things is in the hands of God and He can give

---

[3] Non-Calvinistic Southern Baptists have been using the term "Traditionalist" to describe the most commonly held Southern Baptist view of salvation taught by leaders over the last one hundred years or so. In 2012, a document was produced to better articulate the scholarly non-Calvinistic soteriology of Southern Baptists, whose primary author was Eric Hankins, and was entitled *A Statement of the Traditional Southern Baptist Understanding of God's Plan of Salvation*. The word "traditional" was again used for the basic Baptist view of non-Calvinists. This term has never been meant to suggest that all Southern Baptists have been non-Calvinistic because it is clear there have been two clear streams of soteriology throughout Baptist history. See www.connect316.net for more details.

[4] John Calvin, *Institutes of the Christian Religion*, trans. Henry Beveridge (Grand Rapids: Christian Classics Ethereal Library, 2002), sec. 5, 1030–1031.

life or death at His pleasure, He dispenses and ordains by His judgment that some, from their
mother's womb, are destined irrevocably to eternal death in order to glorify His name in their per-
dition... All are not created on equal terms, but
some are predestined to eternal life, others to
eternal damnation..."5

The very thought of a creator making human beings, with real conscious feelings and emotions, for the
sole purpose of pouring out His everlasting wrath so
as to manifest His glory leaves even Calvinists ponder-
ing.6

The "dreadfulness" of such a decree may accomplish some measure of terror filled "thankfulness" in
the hearts of those who happen to be rescued from this
unthinkable fate, but no one can objectively claim that
they are not on some level troubled by such a doc-
trine.7 If the Scripture clearly teaches us to adopt these
doctrines and the emotional abhorrence that typically
follows, then we certainly must submit ourselves to it.
However, suppose that was not the intention of the
biblical authors at all? Think of what damage such in-

---

5 Gilbert VanOrder, Jr. *Calvinism's Conflicts: An Examination of the
Problems in Reformed Theology* (Lulu Publishers, 2013), 99.

6 Ibid. John Calvin, pg. 124: "How it was ordained by the foreknowledge
and decree of God what man's future was without God being implicated as associate in the fault as the author or approver of transgression, is clearly a secret
so much excelling the insight of the human mind, that I am not ashamed to confess ignorance... I daily so meditate on these mysteries of his judgments that
curiosity to know anything more does not attract me."

7 John Calvin himself admitted the dreadfulness of this teaching: "Again
I ask: whence does it happen that Adam's fall irremediably involved so many
peoples, together with their infant offspring, in eternal death unless because it
so pleased God? Here their tongues, otherwise so loquacious, must become
mute. The decree is dreadful indeed, I confess. Yet no one can deny that God
foreknew what end man was to have before he created him, and consequently
foreknew because he so ordained by His decree." Quote taken from: http://post-
barthian.com/2014/05/31/john-calvin-confessed-double-predestination-hor-
rible-dreadful-decree/; [date accessed: 3/25/15].

terpretations impose upon the church and the believer's view of God if the "dreadfulness" of these doctrines are simply untrue.

Would anyone dare adopt or seek to defend this most troubling doctrine if not for the perceived defense offered by the apostle in Romans 9, for instance? This chapter is by far the most quoted and most debated text of them all with regard to Calvinism's soteriology because it is the only passage that provides any semblance of a defense against the obvious objections these teachings provoke.

But, if it could be shown that the objection Paul is answering in Romans 9 is not in reference to the non-elect reprobate of Calvinism, does that system still have a theological leg upon which to stand? In other words, if it can clearly be shown that the objection Paul is answering is not an objection against the Calvinistic claims, should anyone still seek to defend those claims? I cannot imagine why any believer would want to support these views unless they were thoroughly convinced they are the doctrines being defended by the apostle Paul in this most critical of all Calvinistic proof-texts.

For over a decade, the teachings of Romans 9 were my front line of defense for maintaining my beloved Calvinistic perspective. However, once I saw that Paul's objector was not who I thought him to be, the rest of my defenses toppled under the weight of Calvinism's dreadful claims.

Traditionalists, in contrast to Calvin's quote above, would be more likely to explain soteriology in this manner:

By predestination we mean the predetermined redemptive plan of God to justify, sanctify and glorify whosoever *freely*[8] believes (Rom. 10:11; Jn. 3:16; Eph. 1:1-14). All people are created with equal value as image bearers of God (Jms. 3:9; Gen. 1:27). Because God desires mercy over justice and self-sacrificially loves everyone (Jms. 2:13; Mt. 9:13; 1 Jn. 2:2), He has graciously provided the means of salvation to every man, woman, boy and girl. No person is created for damnation, or predetermined by God to that end (2 Pt. 3:9; 1 Tim. 2:4; Ezek. 18:30-32). Those who perish only do so because they refused to accept the truth so as to be saved (2 Thess. 2:10).[9]

Clearly, there is a stark difference between the two soteriological perspectives:

Calvinists teach that Christ self-sacrificially loves a preselected number of individuals.[10]

Traditionalists teach that Christ loves every single person so much that He died for them all.

Calvinists teach that before the world began, God predestined some individuals to salvation

---

[8] By "freely" we mean libertarian freedom, which is "the ability of the will to refrain or not refrain from a given moral action," not merely the ability to act in accordance with desires that are ultimately determined by God (i.e., "compatibilistic freedom").

[9] For more, see: *A Statement of the Traditional Southern Baptist Understanding of God's Plan of Salvation* by Eric Hankins.

[10] Calvinism is generally known by its unwavering commitment to the soteriology (doctrine of salvation) most popularly represented by the acronym "TULIP" (Total depravity, Unconditional election, Limited atonement, Irresistible grace, and Perseverance of the saints), also referenced as "five points." Some Calvinists call themselves "four pointers" (Amyrauldians), because they reject Limited atonement (the belief that Christ only died for His elect).

and the rest to eternal damnation based on nothing having to do with the individual's choices or
actions.[11]

Traditionalists teach that God has predestined
every individual who is "marked in Christ"
through faith to be saved (Eph. 1:13), and it is each
individual's responsibility to humble themselves
and trust Christ in faith (Lk. 18:8-14).

Before jumping into the proof texts most often
referenced in defense of Calvinism, there are a few
things that should be discussed. In the first chapter we
will reflect on how my understanding of the Potter's
character was turned upside down in my shift away
from Calvinistic thinking.

Then, in chapter 2, we will take a look at the doctrine of Divine election in my journey to better understand the Potter's choices. Yes, that is right, God
makes more than one choice in His redemptive plan to
save the lost.

In chapter 3, we will discuss the biblical doctrine
of divine sovereignty in my journey to understand the
Potter's freedom. Therein, we will expound on what I
believe is the most woefully misunderstood doctrine in
all of Scripture as it relates to soteriology, the doctrine
of "Judicial hardening" (sometimes associated with
what is called the "Messianic secret"). In my experience, very few Calvinists give this doctrine the attention it deserves because it requires a shift in perspective that, if recognized, would undermine their entire
premise.

---

[11] Some Calvinists disagree with Calvin's teaching on double predestination and would argue that God does not predestine the non-elect to damnation, but only the elect to salvation. There are numerous refutations from Calvinistic authors which debunk the inconsistencies of this view.

In chapter 4, we will seek to better understand the Potter's promise (first revealed to Abraham in Genesis 12:3). And in chapter 5, we will go through the three most quoted proof texts of Calvinistic doctrine in my journey to better understand the Potter's word.

In chapter 6, we will look more closely at the Potter's plan followed by the appendix, in which I will answer the Calvinist's most popular argument in defense of their soteriology.

Please approach this study with a willingness to objectively consider whatever current perspective you hold on these issues. Do not allow your heart to be hardened from learning some truth that the Spirit may be presenting through this broken vessel. May the Lord bless you in your studies.

Chapter 1

The Potter's Character

What is God like? What does He want? What are His thoughts? The search to answer these perplexing questions about our eternal Creator has consumed much of my life. Some people can talk about politics or sports for hours on end. Others use their pastime playing golf, fishing or surfing the web. While I've dabbled in all of the above, my hobby, my career, my life's passion has been, in large part, trying to better understand God. I love reading, discussing, listening to and just thinking about anything related to theology. I can never seem to get enough. It is as if the more I learn of God the more I need to know and the more I know of Him the deeper the well is that must be filled.

The Bible uses many analogies to help us better relate to our infinite and mysterious Creator. He is a Father (Mt. 5:48), a faithful Friend (Jn. 15:15), a Shepherd (Ps. 80:1), a Rock (Ps. 18:2), a Bridegroom (Mt. 25:6), and so much more. Believers tend to favor one analogy or another depending on their own needs, experiences and perspective of the world. It is almost as if God knew we would need Him to be our Shepherd at times and our Rock at others. Though He never changes, the way we understand and relate to Him as our God most certainly does.

A number of passages throughout Scripture compare God to a Potter in relation to us, His clay (Is. 29:6, 45:9, 64:8; Jer. 18:1-10; Rom. 9:21). This analogy has meant different things to me throughout my journey in seeking to know Him. At one point, I believed the analogy to mean the Potter seeks to glorify Himself through irresistibly molding vessels to either be objects for wrath or objects for mercy. I agreed with Calvinistic scholars like James White, in his book aptly titled *The Potter's Freedom*, that our Creator sought to display His own glory through either "mercy-ing" some vessels or "hardening" others by His sovereign eternal decree. Or, as John Calvin put it, "...there come from the human race vessels of wrath and vessels of mercy for the manifestation of the glory of God."[12] Calvin taught, and I agreed, that the Potter molded and used His vessels however it suited Him in the pursuit of His ultimate goal of Self-glorification.

Later in life, after personally experiencing God as my redemptive Potter through shameful stumbles and subsequent remolding, I came to understand this analogy in a much different light. I now believe the Scriptures reveal a Potter who manifests His glory by sacrificing Himself for the undeserving vessels, not by making vessels undeserving from birth so as to condemn them to display His glory. I came to realize that God is most glorified not at the expense of His creation, but at the expense of Himself for the sake of His creation.

Allow me to flesh out what I mean by that statement. The God I now see revealed through Christ is one who would rather die than condemn another. He would rather pay the price Himself than make His enemy pay it. He desires mercy over justice (Mt. 5:38-41; Mt. 9:13). He loves His enemies and gives Himself up for them (Mt. 5:43-48). He is like the "good Samaritan" who does not pass by on the other side of the road to avoid His enemies, but instead stops to provide for them even in their rebellion (Lk. 10:25-37). I love Him for that. I want to brag on Him, glorify Him, because

---

[12] John Calvin, *Concerning the Eternal Predestination of God* (Westminster: John Knox Press, 1997), 160.

He is humble at heart and longs for all who are weak to come and find rest in Him (Mt. 11:28-29). I see Jesus as a perfect reflection of the very nature of God. I marvel and boast in the work of Christ because He is not seeking glory for Himself, but for others, and in so doing reveals Himself as the most glorious of all.

He chooses to be born in a barn rather than a mansion; so that one day we can live in a mansion that He prepares for us (Jn. 14:3). He chooses to wash the feet of those who should be washing His, and instead of living a painless life He graciously gives Himself up to death, even death on a cross! That is indeed glorious![13]

When I was a Calvinist, I believed that God's glory was best made manifest through His meticulous control over everything all vessels do,[14] but now I have come to believe, through Christ's example, that His glory is much more evident in His mercy over everything all vessels do (Jn. 12:47, 2 Cor. 5:19). Jesus did not reveal a nature that is in conflict with the triune God, but instead, Jesus corrected misperceptions of God's character that some still hold onto today (Mt. 5; Jms. 1:13-15).

Let me be clear, both Calvinists and non-Calvinists believe God is supremely glorious and desire that His glory is to be made known throughout all the earth. We simply disagree as to how God has freely chosen to go about displaying that glory. Calvinists believe God's glory is best displayed through the attribute of control (typically referred to as "sovereignty"), whereas Traditionalists are convinced, by Christ's revelation, that God's glory is best displayed through the

---

[13] See Philippians 2:1-11 for further insight.

[14] James White wrote, "The conjunction of God's absolute freedom and His Creatorship results in the doctrine of God's decrees: the soul-comforting truth that God has wisely and perfectly decreed whatsoever comes to pass in this universe." James White, *The Potter's Freedom* (Calvary Press, 2000), 45.

attribute of mercy motivated by His genuine self-sacrificial love for all.

What significance does mercy have in a worldview
where there is Divine meticulous control (i.e., "sovereignty") of the sinful desires and choices of each vessel? Is the Potter merely remolding the vessel that He
Himself marred from the beginning by divine decree?
Or, has our Sovereign Potter molded vessels with the
responsibility of choice and graciously provided the
means of redemption for the broken?[15]

Used by God?

I recall attending one of the youth events I oversee
where the praise band was leading the audience in a
song titled, "The Potter's Hand."[16] Along with the stu-
dents, I passionately sang the lyrics, "Take me, Mold
me, Use me..." While there is nothing technically
wrong with these words, something did not sit well. It
was as if the Spirit wanted something more than what
the words were attempting to express in my worship.
I sat down right in the middle of the song and just
started to pray and seek more understanding. I kept
finding myself stuck on the words, "*use me.*"

If one friend says to another, "You were just *using*
me," it would obviously be understood as something
destructive to the relationship. The phrase means that
one person is taking advantage of another for his or
her own selfish motives. If you do not really care about
the other person, but instead are merely "using" them
to accomplish your own desires and purposes then you
cannot rightly be called a "friend." Such attitudes and

---

[15] "Choice" is defined as "the act of picking or deciding between two or
more possibilities." Quote taken from: http://www. merriam- webster.com/-
dictionary/choice; [date accessed: 4/2/15].

[16]Hillsong Music: Lyrics taken from: http://www.azlyrics.comlyrics/-
hillsonglive /thePottershand.html; [date accessed: 4/2/15].

behaviors are destructive to a relationship because they remove trust, joy and mutual love. But, is the concept of being used destructive in our relationship with God? That relationship is different, right? He is almighty God, the Molder in the Heavens who makes and *uses* His clay pots however He pleases to serve His own glory, right? That is what I believed and taught for many years of my ministry. Now, however, I see things a bit differently.

Please understand. I am not attempting to deny that God has every right to mold and use anyone to do whatever He is pleased to have them do. I am not denying God's power or prerogative as God to do anything! I am only questioning His willingness to do so in light of the character I see revealed in Christ. Also, I am not attempting to completely discredit the concept of being used by God, as the lyrics of that song beautifully express. I am not one of those "song police" that feel the need to apply my theological legalese on all songwriters. I am only expressing what I believe God wanted me to see about Him in our own relationship.

Let me illustrate what I mean. When I was a teenager and my dad asked me to do something to help him around the house, I most typically complied while responding, "Yes, sir," because that is how I was raised. I obeyed my dad for one of two reasons: (1) I did not want to get punished or (2) I wanted to get my allowance for the week.

After many years, however, my dad and I have grown to be good friends and even colleagues in ministry. On a rare occasion he will ask me to help him with a chore at his house and I always gladly comply. Why? What motivates me now? I no longer fear his belt (thank God!) nor do I expect any kind of payment. So, why do I happily agree? I love him. He is my friend. Our relationship has matured beyond being motivated by rewards and punishments. He does not merely "*use me*" as his lawn keeper and trash hauler under the threat of punishment or the hope of reward. He confides in me and I confide in him, much like what Jesus seems to be seeking from His own followers,

> **John 15:15:** "No longer do I call you slaves, for the slave does not know what his master is doing; but I have called you friends, for all things that I have heard from My Father I have made known to you."

The night I struggled with the lyrics of that song, I believe that God was seeking to mature our relationship beyond a master/slave mentality and more into a true abiding friendship. He did not want me to ask Him to "*use me*" like I was some object to be discarded once a task was complete. He was seeking intimacy with a child He dearly loves (Rom. 8:15). That still baffles and humbles me to my very core.

God's Character of Love

As a young Calvinist I recall being so annoyed by the emotionally charged rants of some Christians who seemed to think God's only attribute was His love. They would quote John 3:16 at me, as if I had never read it, all the while ignoring the dozens of other passages which speak of His justice and wrath. It infuriated me to no end!

Still to this day I cringe when I hear a non-Calvinist confront a Calvinist with these types of arguments. We need to understand that Calvinists believe that

God is loving and many of them will go to great lengths to even defend His universal love for every person.[17]

With that said, some Calvinistic brethren, when discussing the sincerity of God's love for all people, seem to distance themselves from the logically inevitable conclusions drawn by the implications of their own systematic. While attempting to maintain some semblance of divine love for those unconditionally rejected by God in eternity past, many Calvinists will appeal to God's common provisions such as rain and sunshine. But can such provisions be deemed as *genuinely* loving given the Scripture's own definition of love found in 1 Corinthians 13? Paul, under inspiration of the Holy Spirit, clearly explains *what love is not* when he writes,

> **1 Cor. 13:1-3:** "If I speak in the tongues of men or of angels, but do not have love, I am only a resounding gong or a clanging cymbal. If I have the gift of prophecy and can fathom all mysteries and all knowledge, and if I have a faith that can move mountains, but do not have love, I am nothing. If I give all I possess to the poor and give over my body to hardship that I may boast, but do not have love, I gain nothing."

So we can conclude from Paul's inspired teaching that love is not:

---

[17] See for example a book titled *The Love of God* by John MacArthur who writes, "We must not respond to an overemphasis on divine love by denying that God is love. Our generation's imbalanced view of God cannot be corrected by an equal imbalance in the opposite direction, a very real danger in some circles. I'm deeply concerned about a growing trend I've noticed — particularly among people committed to the biblical truth of God's sovereignty and divine election. Some of them flatly deny that God in any sense loves those whom He has not chosen for salvation. I am troubled by the tendency of some — often young people newly infatuated with Reformed doctrine — who insist that God cannot possibly love those who never repent and believe. I encounter that view, it seems, with increasing frequency." John MacArthur: Quote taken from: http://www. christianity.com /11561793; [date accessed: 4/2/15].

- **Vs. 1:** Having the power to do all things – Omnipotence.
- **Vs. 2:** Having knowledge of all things – Omniscience.
- **Vs. 3:** Providing for the poor and needy – Benevolence.

Omnipotence without love is impotent. Omniscience apart from love is worthless. And even benevolent gifts, like the provisions of rain and sunlight, apart from love are nothing. We know that God is omnipotent, omniscient and graciously benevolent to all humanity, but we also know that these characteristics do not necessarily reflect the true nature of love. God, through his servant, tells *us what true love is:*

1 Cor. 13:4-8: "Love is patient, love is kind. It does not envy, it does not boast, it is not proud. It does not dishonor others, it is not self-seeking, it is not easily angered, it keeps no record of wrongs. Love does not delight in evil but rejoices with the truth. It always protects, always trusts, always hopes, always perseveres. Love never fails."

No Bible believing Christian questions the truth that "God is love" (1 Jn. 4:8). "The Lord is gracious and merciful; Slow to anger and great in loving-kindness. The Lord is good to all, And His mercies are over all His works" (Ps. 145:9). This biblical truth is simply undeniable, which is why some more moderate Calvinists feel the need to offer a rebuttal in defense of God's common love for all people from the obvious implications of the Calvinistic worldview. But, can one objectively conclude that God's treatment of the reprobate within the Calvinistic system is truly "loving" according to God's own definition above?

- Is God patient with the reprobate of Calvinism, who He "hated" and rejected "before he was born or had done anything good or bad?"
- Is God kind to those He destines to torment for all eternity without any regard to their own choices, intentions, or actions?
- Does God honor the non-elect by allowing them to enjoy a little rain and sunlight before they spend an eternity suffering for something with which they had absolutely no control over?
- Is God not easily angered by those who are born under His wrath and without hope of reconciliation?
- Does God keep the record of wrongs committed by reprobates?
- Does the so-called "love" of God for the non-elect fail or does it persevere?

I must ask, as Dave Hunt so succinctly inquired, "What love is this," and by what measure can it ever be deemed "good news!?"[18]

Lest someone accuse me of being uncharitable, it should be noted that some holding to "higher" forms of Calvinism do not even attempt to defend the idea that God sincerely loves everyone. In a work titled, *The Sovereignty of God,* by A.W. Pink, he wrote, "God loves whom He chooses. He does not love everybody." He further argued that the word "world" in John 3:16 ("For God so loved the world...") "refers to the world of believers (God's elect), in contradistinction from 'the world of the ungodly.'"[19]

---

[18] Dave Hunt, *What Love is This? Calvinism's Misrepresentation of God* (The Berean Call, 2006).

[19] Arthur W. Pink, *The Sovereignty of God* (Grand Rapids: Baker, 1930), 29-30.

The issue comes down to how one defines the characteristic of love. According to Paul, "love does not seek its own," and thus it is best described as "self-sacrificial" rather than "self-serving" (1 Cor. 13:5). As Jesus taught, "Greater love has no one than this: to lay down one's life for one's friends." It seems safe to say that love at its very root is self-sacrificial. Anything less than that should not be called "love." One may refer to "kindness" or "care" in reflection of some common provisions for humanity, but unless it reaches the level of self-sacrifice it does not seem to meet the biblical definition of true love.

Given that biblical definition of love as "self-sacrifice," let us consider Christ's command to love our enemies. Is this an expectation Christ Himself is unwilling to fulfill? In other words, is He being hypocritical in this command by telling us to do something He is unwilling to do? Of course not. The very reason He told His followers to love their enemies is "in order that you may be sons of your Father who is in heaven..." (Matt. 5:45).

The meaning is undeniable. We are to love our enemies because God loves His enemies. He loves both "the righteous and the unrighteous" in exactly the same way we are told to love our enemies. The greatest commandment instructs us to "love our neighbor as ourselves" (Lev. 19:18; Matt. 22:37-38). "And who is our neighbor?" (Lk. 10:29). The pagan Samaritans, who were detested as enemies of God. In short, Jesus is teaching us to self-sacrificially love everyone, even our worst enemies, because that reflects the very nature of God Himself.

We know that Jesus perfectly fulfilled the law in every way (Matt. 5:17-18), which would have to include the greatest commandment. Christ's self-sacrificial love for His enemies was certainly as encompassing as what He demanded from His followers in Luke

10. Without a doubt, Jesus loved everyone, even His greatest, most undeserving enemies; otherwise, He would have failed to fulfill the demands of the law.

Paul taught, "For the entire law is fulfilled in keeping this one command: 'Love your neighbor as yourself,'" (Gal. 5:14). And again in Romans 13:8: "He who loves his neighbor has fulfilled the law." Thus, to deny Jesus' self-sacrificial love for everyone is to deny that He fulfilled the demands of the law. This would disqualify Him as the perfect atoning sacrifice.

If we accept that Jesus fulfilled the demands of the law by self-sacrificially loving all people, then how can we conclude that God's love is any less far-reaching than that which is reflected in the Son? Would God expect our love to be more encompassing and self-sacrificial than His own?

When God invites His enemies to be reconciled (Isa. 1:18; 2 Cor. 5:20; Mt. 11:28-30), He is making an appeal from a sincere heart of self-sacrificial love. "'As surely as I live,' declares the Sovereign LORD, 'I take no pleasure in the death of the wicked, but rather that they turn from their ways and live. Turn! Turn from your evil ways! Why will you die, people of Israel?'" (Ezek. 33:11). "The Lord loves the sons of Israel, though they turn to other gods..." (Hosea 3:1). Obviously, God does sincerely love even those who turn from His provision and grace. [20]

With that said, I understand that some have trouble reconciling the idea of God loving His enemies with the following texts:

- **Psalm 5:5:** "You hate all workers of iniquity."

---

[20] John MacArthur, makes a similar argument in his book *The Love of God,* but he redefines love to include the meeting of common needs (such a rain and sunshine), which contradicts Paul's definition in 1 Cor. 13 and undermines his whole argument in defense of God's universal love for humanity.

- **Psalm 7:11:** "God is angry with the wicked every day."
- **Psalm 26:5:** "I have hated the assembly of evil doers."
- **Mal. 1:3 – Rom. 9:13:** "Jacob I have loved, but Esau I have hated."

One must understand that the term "hatred" is sometimes a reflection of "Divine wrath" expressed against those who continue in rebellion, which would not preclude God's longing to see those under wrath come to faith and repentance. Scripture does describe all people being under wrath (and thus "hated" by God) prior to their coming to faith in Christ. This is a point even our Calvinistic brethren affirm. Both Calvinists and Traditionalists teach that all people are by nature under wrath and thus "hated enemies of God" (Eph. 2:3), but we also can affirm together that God does not desire everyone to remain in that condition.

So, in one sense, we can be both hated by God (under His wrath) and loved by God (sought after and provided for). Our point of contention is not whether some are hated and others are loved, but simply how does one go from being under God's wrath (hatred) to being under His provision of grace (love). Is that transition effectually caused by God for a select few, or in light of God's gracious revelation, do all individuals have real responsibility to freely humble themselves in faith?

Further, it should be noted, that the term "hate" is sometimes an expression of choosing one over another for a more honorable purpose, and does not literally mean "hatred" (despise, reject). For instance, Jesus told Peter, "If anyone comes to me and does not hate his own father and mother and wife and children and brothers and sisters, yes, and even his own life, he cannot be my disciple" (Luke 14:26).

No commentator worth his salt would suggest the term "hate" in Luke 14 is literal, otherwise he would be hard pressed to explain Scripture's other teachings about loving and honor our parents. Instead, this passage is rightly understood to mean that man must choose following God's will over the will of even the most beloved in one's life.

Could the same hermeneutical principle be applied toward understanding the biblical references to God's "hatred?" Of course it could. In Romans 9, for instance, Paul may simply be reflecting on God's choice of Jacob (and his posterity) for the honorable purpose of carrying His blessing over his elder brother.

Was not Jacob "by nature [a child] of wrath [hated], just as the others?" (Eph. 2:3). We all should affirm that Jacob remained under wrath [hated] until he came to a point of faith and forgiveness. Even if he came to that point by some "effectual" means, as proposed by the Calvinist, it does not change the fact that he was born under Divine wrath and thus God's "hatred." Therefore, these passages which reflect on God's hatred of some are no more or less troublesome for the non-Calvinistic interpretation.

In an excellent book entitled, *Does God Love Everyone?* Dr. Jerry Walls makes a strong argument for the Divine attribute of love,[21]

> "In a nutshell, our case against Calvinism is that it doesn't do justice to the character of God revealed in Scripture. It does not accurately portray the holy One who is 'compassionate and gracious, slow to anger, abounding in love' (Ps. 103:8), the

---

[21] Jerry Walls, *Does God Love Everyone? The Heart of What's Wrong with Calvinism* (Eugene, OR: Cascade Books, 2016).

God for whom love is not merely an option or sovereign choice, but who is such that his eternal nature is love" (1 Jn 4:8).

Walls makes the case that God's very nature is love, therefore it is not even an option for Him to "not love His creation." For example, we would be repulsed by someone who breeds puppies for the purpose of torturing any of them. Likewise, we would consider it evil for a father or mother to hate any of their own children who they chose to conceive. And, in the same way, it would appear to be evil for God to hate those who He chose to create. Walls argues:

> "God cannot fail to be perfectly loving any more so than He can lie. You don't have to have children, but if you do, you take on an obligation to love them. God's freedom was in the freedom to create, or not. He didn't have to create. But once having created, as a necessarily good and loving Being, He cannot but love what He has created. Love is not an option with God... It's not a question of whether or not God chooses to love, it is WHO HE IS... HE IS LOVE!"

This is not a weakness of God, Walls insists, but His greatest and most self-glorifying *strength*. Would you consider it a strength or a weakness that my character will not allow me to be cruel to my pets?

Is it a weakness that I am unable to willingly strangle one of my own children to death, as Walls argues? No! That is a strength!

God's inability to be unloving is not a shortcoming of God's strength and power, but the greatest most glorifying characteristic of His eternal nature! To declare God's universal self-sacrificial love to the entire world reveals God for what makes Him so abundantly glorious! His love.

Therefore, according to Walls, the question Calvinists are asking is backwards. Instead of asking, as John Piper does, "How does a sovereign God express His love?"[22] We should be asking, "How does a loving God express His sovereignty?"

---

[22] John Piper. Quote taken from: http://www.desiringgod.org/articles/-how-does-a-sovereign-god-love; [date accessed: 12/30/16].

Chapter 2

The Potter's Choices

Notice the title of this chapter is not "The Potter's Election." I considered that title but the reason I went with the word "choices" instead is because the plural form of the word "choice" in English makes the needed distinction more obvious.

That issue may seem insignificant, but it is not if you consider the point of contention in today's soteriological debate over the Calvinistic interpretation of divine election. Many Calvinists, though well intending, have wrongly concluded that the Potter has only one "election" or "choice," and that is for the unconditional, effectual salvation of particular individuals before creation. But, the truth is that our Potter has made several distinct choices in His redemptive plan to ensure the fulfillment of His promise, none of which need involve choosing to effectually save and/or condemn people before the world began.

The 3 Choices of our Kingly Potter

The story that Jesus tells about The Wedding Feast has probably been the most helpful in bringing clarity to the complex issue of divine election in my journey out of Calvinism. Within this narrative there are three different and very distinct choices of God represented. It is my contention that Calvinists have confounded these three choices by treating them as if they are all one and the same. Please allow me to explain and defend this contention carefully and with respect to my fellow brethren.

Take a moment to read the parable of *The Wedding Feast* in Matthew 22:1-14. As you read be sure to note the three distinct choices of our Kingly Potter listed below:

Divine Choice #1: The choice of His servants from within His own country, who were given the task of sending out the invitation.

Divine Choice #2: The choice to send the invitation first to His own country and then to all others.

Divine Choice #3: The choice to allow only those clothed in proper wedding garments to enter into the feast.

The king in this parable clearly represents God and the wedding feast is obviously the kingdom prepared for us. His wedding invitation list includes the people of his own chosen nation, which represents Israel. His servants, people of this same nation, who are called to send out the invitation, clearly represent His prophets and apostles (most of which are mistreated by the other Israelites). Once his own people rejected the invitations, the king chooses to send his chosen messengers to those outside of his own nation, to the "good and bad alike" (vs. 10).

Jesus is giving us a parable that explains how God's elective purposes have come to pass. He chose a people (Israel) to be the nation through which the law, prophets and His Word would be delivered to the entire world (Rom. 3:1-3; 9:4-5). This choice was not based on the impressive size or morality of the nation or its individuals.

Scripture clearly tells us that God did not choose the nation of Israel because it was more impressive

(Deut. 7:7), nor did He choose the individuals from that nation to carry His invitation because they were more moral (Rom. 9:11; Acts 22:3-4). Likewise, the choice to send the message first to the Jews and then the Gentiles does not appear to be based on the morality of those being invited. He plainly states, "The servants went out into the streets and gathered all the people they could find, good and bad alike" (vs. 10).

One might describe these choices as being "unconditional," (as in the Calvinistic concept of "unconditional election"). After all, He did not choose the nation based on its impressiveness, or the individual servants called to carry His invitations based on their morality. Nor does He send the invitations specifically to people who are more moral. So, based on these facts alone, it may appear that God's choices are always unconditional, but the parable is not complete.

Thus far we have only discussed the "many are called" aspects of Christ's parable (Divine Choices #1 and #2), not the "few are chosen," which obviously has to do with individual salvation. Remember, God made numerous choices in bringing the message of redemption (the invitation or the call) to all people. Calvinists jump the gun to presume their premise has been established by pointing to the first two elective purposes of our Kingly Potter throughout Scripture.

In other words, Calvinists point to God's first two elective purposes in bringing the word to the world, which is reflective of His original promise to Abraham, "I will bless all the families of the earth through you" (Gen. 12:3). But, these elective purposes are not about individuals being chosen to salvation. That is reflected in the final choice made by the gracious king.

The kingly choice to save whosoever believes and responds to the divine invitation is seen in the "few" who are "chosen" portion of Christ's parable (Divine Choice #3):

Matt. 22:11-14: "The king went in to look at the guests and saw a man who was not wearing wedding clothes. 'Friend, how did you get in here without wedding clothes?' the king asked him. But the man said nothing. Then the king told the servants, 'Tie him up hand and foot, and throw him outside in the dark. There he will cry and gnash his teeth.' And Jesus concluded, 'Many are invited, but few are chosen.'"

That choice is anything but unconditional. The choice of those who were allowed to eat at the banquet was clearly conditioned upon the individual showing up in the proper clothing. The wedding garments obviously represent being clothed in the righteousness of Christ through faith.[23] The "few" who are "chosen" represent those who responded freely to the invitation sent by the king through his unconditionally chosen servants from his unconditionally chosen nation.

The confusion comes when one convolutes these three distinct choices. For example, does God's choice of Jonah, a servant chosen to carry invitations to Nineveh, equally represent His choice of any particular Ninevite who may respond willingly to this invitation? Does the fact that God uses externally persuasive means, like a storm and big fish, to convince Jonah's rebellious will to obey prove that God uses internally irresistible means (like effectual regeneration) to cause pre-selected Ninevites to respond willingly to Jonah's invitation? If so, the text certainly never draws that conclusion. Why do many Calvinists?

Someone may protest by arguing that Calvinists do not convolute these divine choices in this manner, but many do point to Christ's encounter with Paul on

---

[23] 2 Cor. 5:21; Job 29:14; Is. 11:5, 59:17, 61:10, 64:6; Ps. 132:9; Rev. 3:4, 19:8

the road to Damascus as an example of God's "effectual calling"[24] of some to salvation.[25] Others point to passages, like John 15:16 ("You did not choose me; I chose you..."), as proof texts for the Calvinistic belief of individual election to salvation when clearly Jesus is speaking to His servants who are being prepared to take the invitation to the rest of the world.[26] Calvinists are using Divine Choice #1 as proof for their belief about Divine Choice #3.

In addition, Calvinists often argue that God has "granted repentance or faith" to some individuals but not others, yet clearly such passages represent Divine Choice #2. The king chose to send His invitation first to the Jews (so they may believe and repent) and then to the Gentiles (so that they too may believe and repent). Faith comes by hearing (Rom. 10:17) and thus God is "granting" or "enabling" faith or repentance by sending the invitation to believe and repent.

How can they believe in one whom they have not heard (Rom. 10:14)? How can they come to the banquet without an invitation? By inviting them, He is "granting" them the ability to willingly respond. The concept of God's granting or enabling has never been shown to equal the Calvinistic doctrine of irresistible/effectual calling. A simple definition of the terms reveals that God's enabling mankind to repent is not the same as irresistibly causing repentance.

The church must come to understand God's purpose in electing the nation of Israel to send out His invitation is distinct from His choice to save whosoever

---

[24] "Effectual calling" represents the I of TULIP, sometimes called "Irresistible grace," which is the doctrine that suggests God supernaturally changes the nature of the elect so that they will certainly want to trust in Him.

[25] See John Piper's lesson titled: "God's Sovereignty, Paul's Conversion." http://www.desiringgod.org/articles/gods-sovereignty-pauls-conversion; [date accessed: 3/25/15].

[26] See John Piper's lesson titled: "Five reasons to embrace unconditional election." http://www.desiringgod.org/articles/five-reasons-to-embrace-unconditional-election; [date accessed: 3/25/15].

willingly responds to that invitation, otherwise this doctrine will continue to be a point of confusion and contention.

Chapter 3

The Potter's Freedom

The Potter, in His sovereign freedom, decided to create vessels that bear His image and are free to exercise moral choice, so these earthen vessels from the beginning have fulfilled that decree by making choices between good and evil. When the created vessels choose to do evil, they do not thereby countervail the sovereignty of the Potter, but fulfill it, inasmuch as the Potter decided not which choice His vessels should make but that they should be free to make it. If in His absolute sovereign freedom, the Potter has willed to give His vessels limited freedom, who is there to stay His hand or say, 'What doest thou?' The vessel's will is free because the Potter sovereignly chose to mold His vessel to be free. A Potter less than sovereign could not craft a morally free vessel to bear His image. He would be afraid to do so.[27]

Some seem to believe that for God to be considered "sovereign" then individuals cannot have a libertarian free will.[28] But this view presumes that God, the infinite and omnipotent One, is somehow incapable of

---

[27]Adapted quote from – A.W. Tozer, The Knowledge of the Holy: The Attributes of God (New York: HarperCollins, 1961).

[28] Libertarian free will (sometimes call "Contra-causal" or "autonomous" freedom) is defined as "the categorical ability of the will to refrain or not refrain from any given moral action." Autonomous freedom is not meant to suggest man can be saved apart from the divine work of God, but only that creatures act autonomously or independently of God when choosing moral evil (including their rejection of God's provision). Human autonomy is merely the creaturely side of divine Holiness (i.e., God is separate from all morally evil choices and actions). A defense of human free will is actually a defense of God's Holiness. Contra-causal freedom does not mean mankind is free to do other than what God eternally knows he will do (a finite philosophical speculation), but only that mankind has the moral ability to refrain or not refrain from a morally accountable action. One must not conflate the certainty of God's knowledge with the necessity of human choices.

maintaining sovereignty over libertarianly free creatures; thus this view, while attempting to defend those
very attributes of God, seem to actually undermine
them.

Suppose you went for a walk in your local park
and happened upon an elderly man playing a game of
chess all by himself. You stop and ask him why he is
playing both sides of the chess board, and he says, "It's
the only way I know to guarantee my victory."

You continue on your way to find another elderly
man playing chess with an actual opponent followed
by a line of challengers as far as the eye can see. One
by one they are defeated soundly without much effort
due to the wisdom and abilities of the elderly chess
master. Which one are you going to go home and talk
about? Which one is really greater and more praiseworthy?

Should "sovereignty" be interpreted and understood as the necessity of God to "play both sides of the
chessboard" in order to ensure His victory? Or should
it be understood as God's infinite and mysterious ways
of accomplishing His purposes and ensuring His victory in, through and despite the libertarianly free
choices of creation? Must God be in equal control over
the choices of those who oppose Him in order to accomplish victory? Or is God so powerful, wise, intelligent, all-knowing and infinite in His ability to overcome, work through, and in spite of free evil choices to
accomplish the ultimate good?

One must understand that the attribute of God's
sovereignty, if defined as His providence over creation, is not an eternal attribute. Divine sovereignty is
complete power and authority over all that has been
created. For Him to be in control over others there has
to be others to control. He cannot display His power
over creatures unless the creatures exist. So, before

creation the concept of sovereignty (providential control of the creation) was not an attribute that could be used to describe God. An eternal attribute is something God possesses that is not contingent upon something else existing.

The actual eternal attribute of God in question is His omnipotence, which refers to His eternally limitless power. Sovereignty is a temporal characteristic, not an eternal one, thus we can say God is all-powerful, not because He is sovereign, but He is sovereign because He is all-powerful, or at least He is as sovereign as He chooses to be in relation to this temporal world. Put differently, God is as controlling as He chooses to be over His creation. Sovereignty, therefore, should be described as the expression of God's power, not the source of it.

We can affirm that "God is in heaven; He does whatever pleases Him," (Ps. 115:3) while still holding on to the equally valid truth that, "the highest heavens belong to the Lord, but the earth He has given to mankind" (Ps. 115:16). Traditionalists believe this means that it pleased God to give man a certain level of "autonomy" or "libertarian freedom." It is just a game of question begging for the Calvinist to presume God is pleased to create a world under His meticulous deterministic control (i.e., "sovereignty").

If the all-powerful One chooses to refrain from meticulously ruling over every aspect of that which He creates, that in no way denies His eternal attribute of omnipotence, but indeed affirms it. It is the Calvinist who denies the eternal attribute of omnipotence, by presuming the all-powerful One has no alternative to meticulous deterministic rule over His creation.

In short, the Calvinist denies God's eternal attribute (omnipotence) in his effort to protect the temporal one (sovereignty). Additionally, an argument could be made that the attributes of God's love and His holiness are likewise compromised by the well-meaning efforts of our Calvinistic brethren to protect their concept of deterministic sovereignty over the temporal world.[29]

Look at it this way: which father is more "sovereignly free" in relation to his child? The father whose nature demands that he must use physical force to control the child's every action in order to maintain his physical strength over that child? Or, the father who is freely able to use physical strength or refrain from using physical strength in any given circumstance as he so chooses? Clearly, the latter is more "sovereignly free" because he is not restricted in having to manipulate the child's actions by brute strength.

Arguing that God's nature demands that He remains in meticulous deterministic control over every dust particle and all our moral sinful desires is not an argument in defense of His sovereign freedom, but a repudiation of it.[30]

God, in His freedom, has chosen to give dominion to His creation and He has not yet taken full control over everything on earth as it is in heaven (Mt. 6:10; Ps. 115:16). Passages throughout the Bible teach that there are "authorities" and "powers" which are yet to be destroyed, but have been given limited control.

Isaiah 24:21: "A time is coming when the Lord will punish the powers above and the rulers of the earth."

---

[29] Not all Calvinistic scholars agree on these points. Some may affirm some type of contra-causal freedom of moral creatures. Some affirm such freedom in pre-fallen Adam. For instance, see teaching from Dr. Michael Horton at 43 min mark: https://www.youtube.com/watch?v=1D2SWKbZSIU; [date accessed: 4/23/15].

[30] John Piper said, "Has God predetermined every tiny detail in the universe, such as dust particles in the air and all of our besetting sins? Yes." Quote taken from: http://www.desiringgod.org/ interviews/has-god-predetermined-every-tiny-detail-in-the-universe-including-sin; [date accessed: 4/3/15].

Ephesians 6:12: "For we do not wrestle against flesh and blood, but against the rulers, against the authorities, against the cosmic powers over this present darkness, against the spiritual forces of evil in the heavenly places."

Colossians 2:20: "You have died with Christ, and He has set you free from the evil powers of this world."

1 Corinthians 15:24: "Then the end will come; Christ will overcome all spiritual rulers, authorities, and powers, and will hand over the Kingdom to God the Father."

I am not pretending that we can fully understand His infinite ways or the means by which He accomplishes all things in conjunction with libertarian free will (Deut. 29:29). Frankly, we cannot even understand our own ways, much less His. But, when one considers the revelation of God's holiness (Ezek. 36:23), His unwillingness to even tempt men to sin (James 1:13), His absolute perfect nature and separateness from sin (Is. 48:17; Hab. 1:13), it certainly appears to suggest that our linear, logical constructs should not be used to limit His creative abilities only to the height of our finite imaginations (Is. 55:9).

For example, some argue such things as, "If God knew what would happen in this world prior to creating the world, but chose to create it anyway, then God must have determined everything to be as it is."[31]

---

[31]James White: "How God can know future events, for example, and yet not determine them, is an important point" (Debating Calvinism, p.163). "How could God know it?" asks White. For White, God must determine it, in order to know it. For White, omniscience is simply a matter of God knowing what He scripted, and since God scripted everything, according to White, then it follows that God must then know everything. White writes: "How can God know what

While the logic of this sounds plausible, we must recognize the limitations inherent within such finite observations. The argument imposes a linear way of thinking, and a cause/effect construct upon an infinite Being, who is not bound by time, space, cause and effects. His ways are higher than our ways and so we cannot presume that His knowledge of future events is somehow equal to what our knowledge of future events might be if we had a crystal ball and could somehow look through the linear corridors of time.

What do we know of the eternal dimension or the knowledge contained therein? How do we measure God's infinite ways and dogmatically assume a causal link between what is known in eternity and what happens temporally? Does God know it because He determines it or does He determine it because He knows it? Or maybe He permits others to make determinations separately (autonomously)?

When speaking of God, why is the term "foreknowledge" even employed by the inspired biblical authors if a more applicable term like "predetermine" is available and better suited? If He determines all things that come to pass, then what purpose is there in speaking of His mere knowledge or permitting of anything? Why does such language even exist in Scripture if exhaustive determinism is true? There is no good reason to ever speak of God merely knowing or enabling anything in such a worldview, as such terminology would only serve to placate reality.

John Calvin forthrightly reveals where his own systematic leads:

---

these free creatures will do in the future, if they are truly free?" (Debating Calvinism, p.168) It's clear that White doesn't believe that God could know what free creatures would do, unless God determined their actions. Quotes taken from: www.examiningcalvinism.com; [date accessed: 3/15/15].

"A distinction has been invented between doing and permitting, because to many it seemed altogether inexplicable how Satan and all the wicked are so under the hand and authority of God, that He directs their malice to whatever end He pleases, and employs their iniquities to execute His judgments...

How foolish and frail is the support of divine justice afforded by the suggestion that evils come to be, not by His will but by His permission... *It is a quite frivolous refuge to say that God otiosely permits them, when Scripture shows Him not only willing, but the author of them...*Who does not tremble at these judgments with which God works in the hearts of even the wicked whatever He will, rewarding them nonetheless according to desert? Again it is quite clear from the evidence of Scripture that God works in the hearts of men to incline their wills just as He will, whether to good for His mercy's sake, or to evil according to their merits."[32]

Many modern day Calvinists would not go so far as to candidly admit what John Calvin does in the quote above. Yet, can the Calvinistic systematic avoid the necessity of this logical end? Their namesake does not think so.

Certain philosophical commitments led John Calvin and many Calvinists to adopt a view of God that is not biblically defensible. Our infinite God is not stuck on a linear timeline, looking into the past or the future. He is the timeless great "I AM," which suggests that His knowledge is less like our set knowledge of past events (or future ones if we had a crystal ball) and

---

[32] John Calvin, *The Eternal Predestination of God*; 10:11. [emphasis added.]

more like our knowledge of present reality. We know what is happening right *now* because we exist in the *now,* not because we are necessarily determining what we are experiencing in the *here and now,* though our choices and actions could certainly affect our present reality.

Likewise, our infinite God exists in the *eternal now,* which is beyond our comprehension. Should we (indeed can we) draw dogmatic conclusions about such infinite realities? Should we conclude that God determines the evils of this world with the same "sovereignty" that determined the redemption by which those evils are reconciled?

Is God determining to merely correct His own determinations? I have to believe it is a bit more complex than that. There is nothing that impressive about a deterministic worldview; after all, even a good computer programmer can create a deterministic virtual world. Certainly our omnipotent God is more creative and complex than what can be manufactured by the most intelligent deterministic philosopher's imagination.

To us the past is unchangeable - water under the bridge. The future, however, is as uncertain as the forecast of rain and impossible for us to fully predict or know. The only point where the "changeable" meets "certainty" for us is in the present. But, is that also true of our infinite Creator? What if the past, present and future remains both certain and changeable to God? As some have put it, "God is in the eternal now."

C.S. Lewis aptly wrote in his book *Mere Christianity,* "If you picture time as a straight line along which we have to travel, then you must picture God as the whole page on which the line is drawn." He argues that all times are the present to God insomuch as His knowledge is concerned. Other philosophers contend that God must be either outside of time or in time, whereas Lewis argues,

"Why can't it be both? There is no logical barrier to this. Just because there is no creature in our experience that is both inside and outside of time, does not mean God has to be like His creatures."[33]

Wherever we land philosophically, however, we must refrain from bringing unbiblical conclusions based upon our finite perceptions to our understanding of God's nature.[34] We must accept the revelation of Scripture. He is Holy (Is. 6:3). He does not take pleasure in sin (Ps. 5:4). Some moral evil does not even enter His Holy mind (Jer. 7:31). And, He genuinely desires all men, every individual, to come to Him and be saved (Rom. 10:21; 2 Pet. 3:9; 1 Tim. 2:4; Ezek. 18:30-31).

One presumption that we should bring to Scripture is that our God is good and He is in no way implicit in the bringing about of moral evil. He is a loving God who genuinely desires for all to come to repentance so as to be saved (2 Pet. 3:9).

No man will stand before the Father and be able to give the excuse, "I was born unloved by my Creator (Jn. 3:16). I was born un-chosen and without the hope of salvation (Titus 2:11). I was born unable to see, hear or understand God's revelation of Himself (Acts 28:27-28)." No! They will stand wholly and completely "without excuse" (Rm. 1:20), because God loved them (Jn. 3:16), called them to salvation (2 Cor. 5:20), revealed Himself to them (Titus 2:11), and provided the

---

[33] C.S. Lewis, *Mere Christianity* (Touchstone Books, 1943), 147.
    One would also benefit from reading *The Consolation of Philosophy* (Latin: De consolatione philosophiæ), a work by the sixth-century philosopher Boethius that has been described as having had the single most important influence on the Christianity of the Middle Ages and early Renaissance and as the last great work of the Classical Period. *Introduction to The Consolation of Philosophy*, (Oxford World's Classics, 2000).
    [34] Deut. 29:29 states, "The secret things belong to the LORD our God, but the things revealed belong to us and to our sons forever..."

means by which their sins would be atoned (1 Jn. 2:2). No man has any excuse for unbelief (Rm. 1:20).

Chapter 4

The Potter's Promise

The Potter had a vessel named Abram. He told him to leave his home and go to a new land. Before he left, the Potter made Abram a very important promise. He said:

Gen. 12:2-3: "And I will make you a great nation, And I will bless you, And make your name great; And so you shall be a blessing; And I will bless those who bless you, And the one who curses you I will curse. And in you all the families of the earth will be blessed."

The Potter always, and I mean always, keeps His promises. Even when the vessels went their own way and ignored the instructions of the Potter, He remained faithful to His promise.

How could a nation be made great if the vessels within it refuse to obey? How can a nation bless all the families of earth if they refuse to listen to the instructions of the Potter? A lesser Potter would trash such a spoiled lump of clay, but not this Potter. He remains faithful to His promise even when the clay is unfaithful. But how? How does the Potter do it? I suppose the Potter could mold clay without any real freedom to make choices between available moral options and simply shape it to desire to do what the Potter wants it to do. But is that what Scripture reveals?

What tools are in the Potter's workshop to handle free vessels that do not obey? Does the Bible give us insight into how the Potter works with His free vessels to bring about His plan in order to fulfill His promise?

Indeed, it does. But, be warned, the Potter's ways are much higher than that of the clay and "He is too good to be unkind and He is too wise to be mistaken. And when we cannot trace His hand, we must trust His heart."[35]

The tools of the Potter are mysterious, but Scripture does give us some insight into His ways. Let us seek to understand our gracious Potter more clearly.

The Messianic Secret

> **Mark 9:9:** "As they were coming down the mountain, Jesus gave them orders not to tell anyone what they had seen until the Son of Man had risen from the dead."

> **Matt. 16:20:** "Then He warned His disciples not to tell anyone that He was the Christ."

> **Mark 3:12:** "But he gave them strict orders not to tell who He was."

> **Mark 8:30:** "Jesus warned them not to tell anyone about Him."

These passages certainly seem to suggest that Jesus had a secret. Some scholars refer to Jesus' use of parabolic language (Matt. 13; Mark 4; John 6:26-71) and His warnings not to tell others that He was the Christ (Matt. 16:20; Mark 1:24-25, 34, 43-45; 3:12; 8:30; 9:9) as the *Messianic secret*. This addresses Je-

---

[35] Charles Spurgeon: "God is too good to be unkind and He is too wise to be mistaken. And when we cannot trace His hand, we must trust His heart." Quote taken from: http://www.goodreads.com/quotes/ta-g/charles-spurgeon; [date accessed: 4/3/15].

sus' expressed desire to keep His "messiah-ness" se-cret at times while here in the flesh.[36] *The Handbook on Biblical Criticism* states,

> "Messianic secret refers to a discernible phenom-enon in the Gospels, most especially in the Gospel of Mark, in which Jesus explicitly conceals His Messianic character and power until the closing period of His ministry."[37]

The *Messianic secret*, if rightly understood, is not Jesus' attempt to permanently keep people from knowing, believing in, and following Him. Instead, it is the temporary strategy Jesus employed to accom-plish redemption on Calvary so that all may be saved through faith in Him after His plan was fulfilled. As the apostle Paul noted:

> **1 Cor. 2:8-9:** "We speak of God's secret wisdom, a wisdom that has been hidden and that God des-tined for our glory before time began. None of the rulers of this age understood it, for if they had, they would not have crucified the Lord of glory."

Jesus knew that had they believed in Him before the right time then they would not have crucified Him. Therefore, the Lord graciously taught in parables "to those on the outside... so that, 'they may be ever seeing but never perceiving, and ever hearing but never un-derstanding; otherwise they might turn and be for-given!'" (Mark 4:11b-12). As Paul noted, "God's secret

---

[36] This purposeful hiding of divine revelation is also referred to as "Judi-cial hardening" or "blinding" of already calloused and rebellious individuals. Richard N. Soulen and R. Kendall Soulen, ed. *The Handbook on Biblical Criti-cism (4th ed.).* (Louisville: Westminster John Knox Press, 2011), 124.

wisdom...has been hidden" but He has done this for "our glory."

John 6 is one of the most referenced chapters in the discussion over mankind's God-given abilities to respond willingly to the gospel appeal. Unfortunately, the issue of the "Messianic secret" (or what I have referred to as "Judicial hardening" discussed later) has been virtually ignored in many modern theological circles leading to false interpretations of these contested passages.

What is known about the Israelites of this day? Scripture reveals that they have "become calloused...otherwise they might see with their eyes, hear with their ears, understand with their hearts and turn, and I would heal them" (Acts 28:27). They were not born calloused, but over time they had grown hardened in their religious self-righteousness, which prevented them from hearing, seeing and responding to the revelation of God.

At this vital time in human history, they are being "judicially hardened" or "cut off" (Rom. 9:1-3) or "sent a spirit of stupor" (Rom. 11:8) so as to seal them in their already calloused condition (John 12:39-41; Acts 28:27). Scripture tells us that God is hardening the calloused Jews in order to accomplish a greater redemptive purpose through their rebellion. It is God's ordained plan to bring redemption to the world through the crucifixion of the Messiah by the hands of the rebellious Jews (Acts 2:23).

Jesus is not attempting to persuade everyone to come to faith in great numbers as we see following Pentecost when Peter preaches (Acts 2:41). In fact, quite the opposite seems to be the case. To accomplish the redemptive plan through Israel's unbelief, we see Jesus actively instructing His apostles not to tell others who He is yet (Matt. 16:20; Mark 8:30; 9:9).

Moreover, Jesus purposefully speaks in riddles in order to prevent the Jewish leaders coming to faith and repentance (Matt. 13:11-15; Mark 4:11-13). When great numbers began to believe Jesus was truly prophetic, notice how Jesus responded: "'Surely this is the Prophet who is to come into the world.' Jesus, knowing that they intended to come and make him king by force, withdrew again to a mountain by Himself" (John 6:14-15).

Earlier in the same gospel we learn that "many people saw the miraculous signs He was doing and believed in His name. But Jesus would not entrust Himself to them..." (John 2:23b-24a). John later reveals this has been a key part of God's redemptive plan all along:

> **John 12:37-40:** "Even after Jesus had done all these miraculous signs in their presence, they still would not believe in him. This was to fulfill the word of Isaiah the prophet: 'Lord, who has believed our message and to whom has the arm of the Lord been revealed?' *For this reason, they could not believe*, because, as Isaiah says elsewhere: 'He has blinded their eyes and deadened their hearts, so they can neither see with their eyes, nor understand with their hearts, nor turn— and I would heal them'" (emphasis added).

For what reason could they not believe? Is it because they were rejected by their Maker before the world began? Is it about their being born guilty of Adam's sin and thus incapable of responding willingly to God's own appeals for reconciliation? Of course not! They are being temporarily blinded in their already calloused condition so as to accomplish redemption for the world. This is not about God rejecting most of humanity before the world began as the Calvinistic systematic reads into these texts.

Why Riddles?

> **Mark 4:11-12, 33-34:** "The secret of the kingdom of God has been given to you. But to those on the outside everything is said in parables so that, 'they may be ever seeing but never perceiving, and ever hearing but never understanding; *otherwise they might turn and be forgiven!*' ...With many similar parables Jesus spoke the word to them, as much as they could understand. *He did not say anything to them without using a parable.* But when He was alone with His own disciples, He explained everything" (emphasis added).

Clearly, Jesus used riddles, or parables, to keep the Jewish leaders in the dark for a time so as to accomplish a greater redemptive good. This completely undermines Calvinism's doctrine of "Total Inability." There is no practical or theological reason for God to put a blindfold on those born totally and completely blind from birth. And there is certainly no reason to hide truth from those in the "corpse-like dead" condition of "Total Inability" proposed by the "T" in Calvinism's TULIP.

Judicial Hardening

The doctrine of God's Judicial hardening is crucial in rightly understanding much of the biblical teachings regarding election, predestination and salvation. A misunderstanding or lack of clarity regarding this one doctrine will lead to many more serious misapplications of Scripture.

As a former Calvinist, I can think of no greater point of contention in my struggle over these doctrines than rightly defining God's active role in judicially hardening Israel from recognizing their own Messiah (especially as it relates to understanding the often referenced proof texts of Romans 9 and John 6).

When it comes to God's sovereign control over moral evil, as reflected in the pages of Scripture, there is no shortage of confusion and controversy within the church. There are typically three main examples presented in this discussion:

1) **Joseph being sold by his brothers into slavery:** "You intended to harm me, but God intended it for good to accomplish what is now being done, the saving of many lives" (Gen. 50:20).

2) **Pharaoh hardened by God to accomplish the Passover:** "But the LORD hardened Pharaoh's heart and he would not listen to Moses and Aaron, just as the LORD had said to Moses" (Ex. 9:12).

3) **The Crucifixion of Jesus:** "This man was handed over to you by God's deliberate plan and foreknowledge; and you, with the help of wicked men, put Him to death by nailing Him to the cross...They did what your power and will had decided beforehand should happen" (Acts 2:23; 4:28).

All Christian scholars can agree that God at least allowed sinful actions to take place for a greater plan and purpose. We can also all agree that God's involvement was completely sinless. We could simply stop there and appeal to the mystery as to how God works in such instances, but philosophers are going to do what philosophers are going to do: philosophize. And as C.S. Lewis states, "Good philosophy must exist, if for no other reason, because bad philosophy needs to be answered."[38]

Speaking of "bad philosophy," some have theorized that because God is "meticulously deterministic" (i.e., "sovereign") in the examples listed above, then He must be "meticulously deterministic" in every instance of all time. For example, John Hendryx, a compatibilistic philosopher from monergism.com, speculates:

> "In order to understand this better, theologians have come up with the term 'compatibilism' to describe the concurrence of God's sovereignty and man's responsibility. *Compatibilism is a form of determinism and it should be noted that this position is no less deterministic than hard determinism.* It simply means that God's predetermination and meticulous providence is 'compatible' with voluntary choice [choosing according to one's desire]. Our choices are not coerced ...i.e., we do not choose against what we want or desire, yet we never make choices contrary to God's sovereign decree. What God determines will always come to pass (Eph. 1:11).
>
> In light of Scripture, (according to compatibilism), *human choices are exercised voluntarily but the desires and circumstances that bring about these choices occur through divine determinism.* For example, God is said to specifically ordain the crucifixion of His Son, and yet evil men willfully and voluntarily crucify Him (see Acts

---

[38] C. S. Lewis, *Learning in War-Time, in The Weight of Glory and Other Addresses* (Orlando, FL: Macmillan, 1980), 28.

2:23 & 4:27-28). This act of evil is not free from God's decree, but it is voluntary, and these men are thus responsible for the act, according to these texts. Or when Joseph's brothers sold him into slavery in Egypt, Joseph later recounted that what his brothers intended for evil, God intended for good (Gen 50:20). God determines and ordains that these events will take place (that Joseph will be sold into slavery), yet the brothers voluntarily make the evil choice that brings *[sic]* it to pass, which means the sin is imputed to Joseph's brothers for the wicked act, and God remains blameless. In both of these cases, it could be said that God ordains sin, sinlessly. *Nothing occurs apart from His sovereign good pleasure... Our choices are our choices because they are voluntary, not coerced. We do not make choices contrary to our desires or natures, nor separately from God's meticulous providence. Furthermore, compatibilism is directly contrary to contra-causal free will [or libertarian free will]. Therefore voluntary choice is not the freedom to choose otherwise...*"[39]

In this theory, God is involved at the level of determining men's evil desires in such a manner that they could not have refrained from the given moral action (see the italicized portions above). In other words, Hendryx supposes that God brings these evil events about by meticulously determining all the circumstances and the evil desires of man. Hendryx denies that people ever have the ability of making libertarianly free choices (the ability of the will to refrain or not refrain from a given moral action). Instead, Hendryx

---

[39] Quote taken from link sent to the author by Phil Johnson (President of Grace to You Ministries) via Twitter: http://www.monergism.com/the-threshold/articles/onsite /qna/sovereignfree.html; [date accessed 12/14/14]. emphasis added.

is arguing that man is acting in accordance with the desires and circumstances that God has meticulously determined.

Calvinistic author and pastor, John Piper, quotes from Mark Talbot in order to explain this same point:

> "God...brings about all things in accordance with His will. In other words, it isn't just that God manages to turn the evil aspects of our world to good for those who love Him; it is rather that He Himself brings about these evil aspects for His glory (see Ex. 9:13-16; John 9:3) and His people's good (see Heb. 12:3-11; James 1:2-4). This includes—as incredible and as unacceptable as it may currently seem—God's having even brought about the Nazis' brutality at Birkenau and Auschwitz as well as the terrible killings of Dennis Rader and even the sexual abuse of a young child..."[40]

Mark Talbot, John Piper, and all those associated with this publication, are teaching that God actually *brings about the sexual abuse of children* in order to glorify Himself, yet He does so without sinning. In other words, they believe that God does these seemingly horrible things while somehow not being held culpable. How can that be? How can God meticulously and purposefully bring about child molestation for His glory while avoiding culpability? No consistent Calvinist has ever provided an answer to this question. In fact, John Calvin honestly admits the difficulty of this dilemma:

---

[40] Mark R. Talbot, "All the Good That Is Ours in Christ: Seeing God's Gracious Hand in the Hurts Others Do to Us," John Piper and Justin Taylor (eds.), *Suffering and the Sovereignty of God* (Wheaton: Crossway, 2006), 31-77.

"How it was ordained by the foreknowledge and decree of God what man's future was without God being implicated as associate in the fault as the author or approver of transgression, is clearly a secret so much excelling the insight of the human mind, that I am not ashamed to confess ignorance...I daily so meditate on these mysteries of His judgments that curiosity to know anything more does not attract me."[41]

Similarly, John MacArthur, a notable Calvinistic pastor, was asked the question, "If God literally brings about everything then how can He blame me for sinning?" He answered, "I don't know the answer to that, and I don't know of anyone who knows the answer to that."[42]

Hendryx's intentions, like that of these other Calvinistic scholars, are noble because they clearly strive to maintain that God remains sinless in all His dealings, but I believe the compatibilist's theory falls short in accomplishing that goal.[43]

James 1:13 teaches, "When tempted, no one should say, 'God is tempting me.' For God cannot be tempted by evil, nor does He tempt anyone." Yet, would Calvinists have us believe that God refrains from tempting, but somehow determines the very desires of the tempter and the tempted so as to necessitate the sinful action in every circumstance? This the-

---

[41] John Calvin, *Concerning the Eternal Predestination of God* (London: James Clarke and Co., 1961), 124.

[42] John MacArthur, Question and Answer at Grace to You. Quote taken from: https://www.youtube.com/watch?v=3Pr9aHEBfRU; [date accessed 12/14/14].

[43] We believe Calvinists are attempting to maintain a blatant contradiction (A = not A) in claiming that God is responsible for moral evil while not being held responsible for moral evil.

ory simply cannot be supported from the whole counsel of Scripture. Please allow me to propose another theory.[44]

Traditionalists believe that at times throughout history God does intervene to determine some things. That is what makes these things "of God" and uniquely supernatural (i.e., redemption on Calvary or the inspiration of Scripture). I also believe God may use means similar to what some Calvinists speculate in these instances. I do not believe, however, these unique determinations prove God's meticulous determination of all things, especially mankind's evil intentions. In fact, in every one of the instances listed above the purpose of God's unique intervention is clearly redemptive. I refuse to believe God is merely seeking to redeem the very evil intentions and actions that He Himself brought to pass by "meticulous determinism." God is not merely determining to clean up His other determinations. He is cleaning up mankind's libertarianly free choices and actions.

Anticipated Objection:
The Accusation of Misrepresentation

Do Calvinists really affirm the universal divine causal determinism of every single thing that comes to pass, including heinous moral evil?

It is not uncommon for a Calvinist to tell me that they feel I am misrepresenting Calvinism because I speak of it as if it is "too deterministic." For instance,

---

[44] Notice that I call it a theory and refrain from speaking with dogmatism and authoritative certainty about matters where Scripture is not abundantly clear. Also, notice that Hendryx and I share the same exact goal. We both desire to explain, from Scripture, how God works in relation to moral evil while remaining sinless. Hendryx is not a heretic. I'm not angry with him. He is working with good intentions to best reflect what he believes Scripture is revealing. He should be admired for such effort. I simply believe his speculations go too far and thus do not adequately reflect the revelation of God in Scripture.

Calvinistic apologist Matt Slick, in an online debate, told me that he did not believe in determinism only later to affirm the statement referenced above from monergism.com which states, *"compatibilism is no less deterministic than hard determinism."*

Dr. William Lane Craig, a leading non-Calvinistic Christian apologist, regularly describes Calvinism as "universal divine causal determinism," which he defines as meaning, "God determines everything that happens in the world." One listener brought a similar critique to Dr. Craig:

> "I believe you really mischaracterize Calvinism. What you are talking about sounds more like Hyper-Calvinism. Because Calvinism actually does affirm free will; I can read chapter 10 of the Westminster Confession of Faith where it actually explains how free will works within that system."

Dr. Craig answered by saying:

> "What I am rejecting is universal divine causal determinism. Now, if Reformed theology rejects compatibilism then I have got no quarrel with it. In fact, when I read much of the Westminster Confession, I resonate with it. The problem is that I don't think that the Reformed theologian can give us a coherent interpretation of Scripture. As I said, the Reformed divines – in my first point – typically say that the reconciliation of these texts is just inscrutable. They can't put them together; it is a mystery."[45]

---

[45]Transcript of William Lane Craig's Defenders 2 class: Quote taken from: http://www.reasonablefaith .org /defenders-2-podcast/transcript/s8-10#ixzz486DZNR4F [accessed online: 12/17/15].

What many Calvinists seem to miss is that compatibilism, the philosophical system adopted by most notable scholars leading in the resurgence of Calvinism today, is a form of hard determinism. It is the belief that God's determinism of all things (sometimes referenced as "sovereignty" or "meticulous providence") is compatible with "creaturely freedom" (defined as creatures acting in accordance with their divinely decreed nature/desires).

My arguments, like those of Dr. Craig, simply do not pertain to those Calvinists who deny "universal divine causal determinism" (i.e., compatibilism). However, it must be recognized that the group with which many associate called "Calvinism" is being led by those who do affirm "universal divine causal determinism," just like the namesake theologian of this systematic, John Calvin. Consider Calvin's own words:

> "Creatures are so governed by the secret counsel of God, that nothing happens but what He has knowingly and willingly decreed" (John Calvin, *Institutes of Christian Religion*, Book 1, Chapter 16, Paragraph 3).

> "...thieves and murderers, and other evildoers, are instruments of divine providence, being employed by the Lord Himself to execute judgments which He has resolved to inflict" (John Calvin, *Institutes of Christian Religion*, Book 1, Chapter 17, Paragraph 5).

> "We hold that God is the disposer and ruler of all things, –that from the remotest eternity, according to His own wisdom, He decreed what He was to do, and now by His power executes what He decreed. Hence we maintain, that by His provi-

dence, not heaven and earth and inanimate creatures only, but also the counsels and wills of men are so governed as to move exactly in the course which He has destined" (John Calvin, *Institutes of Christian Religion*, Book 1, Chapter 16, Paragraph 8).

"The devil, and the whole train of the ungodly, are in all directions, held in by the hand of God as with a bridle, so that they can neither conceive any mischief, nor plan what they have conceived, nor how muchsoever they may have planned, move a single finger to perpetrate, unless in so far as He permits, nay unless in so far as He commands, that they are not only bound by His fetters but are even forced to do Him service" (John Calvin, *Institutes of Christian Religion*, Book 1, Chapter 17, Paragraph 11).

"Many professing a desire to defend the Deity from an individual charge admit the doctrine of election, but deny that any one is reprobated. This they do ignorantly and childishly, since there could be no election without its opposite, reprobation" (John Calvin, *Institutes of Christian Religion*, Book 3, Chapter 23, Paragraph 1).

"...it is utterly inconsistent to transfer the preparation for destruction to anything but God's secret plan... God's secret plan is the cause of hardening" (John Calvin, *Institutes of Christian Religion*, Book 2, Chapter 23, Paragraph 1).

"I admit that in this miserable condition wherein men are now bound, all of Adam's children have fallen by God's will" (John Calvin, *Institutes of*

Christian Religion, Book 3, Chapter 23, Paragraph 4).

"With Augustine I say: the Lord has created those whom He unquestionably foreknew would go to destruction. This has happened because He has willed" (John Calvin, *Institutes of Christian Religion*, Book 3, Chapter 23, Paragraph 5).

"...individuals are born, who are doomed from the womb to certain death, and are to glorify Him by their destruction" (John Calvin, *Institutes of Christian Religion*, Book 3, Chapter 23, Paragraph 6).

"...it is vain to debate about prescience, which it is clear that all events take place by His sovereign-appointment" (John Calvin, *Institutes of Christian Religion*, Book 3, Chapter 23, Paragraph 6).

"But since He foresees future events only by reason of the fact that He decreed that they take place, they vainly raise a quarrel over foreknowledge, when it is clear that all things take place rather by His determination and bidding" (John Calvin, *Institutes of Christian Religion*, Book 3, Chapter 23, Paragraph 6).

"Again I ask: whence does it happen that Adam's fall irremediably involved so many peoples, together with their infant offspring, in eternal death unless because it so pleased God? The decree is dreadful indeed, I confess. Yet no one can deny that God foreknew what end man was to have before He created him, and consequently foreknew because He so ordained by His decree. And it ought not to seem absurd for me to say that God not only foresaw the fall of the first man, and in him the ruin of his descendants, but also meted it out in accordance with His own decision" (John Calvin, *Institutes of Christian Religion*, Book 3, Chapter 23, Paragraph 7).

"The first man fell because the Lord deemed it meet that He should" (John Calvin, *Institutes of Christian Religion*, Book 3, Chapter 23, Paragraph 8).

Now, before moving on, I hope all those who proudly wear the label "Calvinist" can rightly understand what I am opposing here. I have not misrepresented or "straw-manned" Calvinism. John Piper is arguably the most influential modern day proponent of Calvinism and he is representing exactly what John Calvin himself taught on this subject in the quotes above (all of which are properly cited for contextual examination). Both of these Calvinistic scholars are abundantly clear about what they believe.

I am not suggesting a "Calvinist" must agree with John Piper or even John Calvin on every theological point in order to be considered a "Calvinist." But if you are going to proudly promote this label shouldn't you at least affirm the basic theological claims over the issues that make Calvinism so controversial in the church?

The major reason we even know of John Calvin and "Calvinism" is because of his controversial views over predestination, election, free will, and sovereignty. If you cannot affirm his statements on at least those issues, then may I suggest you stop promoting the label "Calvinist?" Or, if nothing else, at least stop accusing people, like myself, of not really understanding Calvinism?

Hardening

How does God bring about His purposes while remaining sinless if not in the manner the Compatibilist supposes? The answer to this question goes back to the doctrine of Judicial hardening (and the Messianic secret) discussed earlier. To be clear on this point, there are two kinds of hardening taught in Scripture:

Self-hardening: This is where a morally accountable person, who is able to refrain or not refrain from given moral actions (libertarianly free), grows stubborn or calloused in his own ways.[46]

Judicial hardening: This is God's active role in blinding an already rebellious person in their rebellion so as to prevent their repentance for a time. God's motive is ALWAYS to accomplish a greater redemptive purpose through their rebellious actions (often including the potential redemption even of those being judicially hardened).[47]

---

[46] Baker's Evangelical Dictionary of Biblical Theology: *Hardening, Hardness of Heart*: "Self-Hardening of the heart goes beyond the tragic obtuseness of our inherited condition in the Fall of man. Working on the fertile soul of our innately immoral hearts, the act of sinning hardens the heart into a stubborn rebellion against all that is good. So, people may harden their own hearts, in sinful rebellion, in bitterness, or in sheer self-will. (Zech. 7:11-13; Ex. 9:34-35; 2 Chron. 36:13; Zech. 7:12; Dan. 5:20; Eph. 4:18; Heb. 3:12-15)" Quote taken from: http://www.biblestudytools.com/dictionaries/bakersevangelicaldictionary/hardening-hardness-of-heart.html; [date accessed: 11/15/14].

[47] Ibid: "Judicial hardening – In a few instances such as Pharaoh and the Egyptians (Ex. 7:3; 9:12), Sihon, king of Heshbon (Deut. 2:30), and the Hivites living in Gibeon (John 11:19-20), it is said that God hardened their hearts. Apparently these people were so irremediable in their rebellion against God that God entered into the hardening process so that he could accomplish His purposes in spite of, and yet in and through, that hardness. It is God's prerogative, as God, to do this (Rom. 9:18-21). That they are morally responsible for their condition is a theological given, and we are warned not to harden our hearts as they did, a command that would make no sense if hardening were simply God's act (1 Sam. 6:6). Israel's hardening as a nation was an act of self-

Judicial hardening is simply hiding or confusing the revelation of truth that could otherwise lead to repentance, like when Jesus spoke using riddles (Mark 4:11-12; Rom. 11:8). So God is not said to have caused or enticed anyone. He simply lets a man continue down his self-hardened path and ensures that no revelation is clear enough to convince him to repent prior to the sovereign redemptive purpose being served by his free acts of rebellion (like when the Jews cried out "crucify Him!").

Consider this analogy: When a police officer sets up a speed trap, he has one ultimate desire: to slow down speeders for the safety of all. However, by hiding the truth of his presence he is ensuring that those who want to speed will continue to do so. Thus, in one sense he wants the speeders to continue to speed so as to catch them speeding, but his ultimate purpose is the same: to slow down speeders for the safety of all. The police officer does not determine the speeders desire to speed in any way, he simply hides the truth so as to ensure the speeders will continue to speed, something they have freely chosen to do. Never is the will of the officer in conflict with his good purpose.

Let's look at another analogy. Suppose my 4-year-old daughter was told that she is not to take cookies from the cookie jar. In another room, out of sight, I see into the kitchen that my daughter is looking at the cookie jar. She looks around the room to see if anyone is watching. As a parent, I can tell what she is thinking. She is about to steal a cookie and she knows it is forbidden.

Now, I could step into the room so that she sees me prior to her committing this sin. Upon seeing me

---

hardening followed by God's act of Judicial hardening as clearly portrayed in the Scripture (Matt. 23:37; Rom. 10-11)."

she would forego her evil plot and give up the idea of getting the cookie (at least until the next time she was alone). However, suppose I decide to not step into the room. I remain out of sight to allow her to be tempted and then pounce into action to catch her with her hand in the cookie jar.

By not stepping in at the moment I saw she was being tempted, did I cause the temptation? No. I allowed it to continue, but I did not cause it. I did not determine for her to desire to steal. I could have prevented the action by simply showing myself, but I chose not to do so.

This is similar to what God is doing with Judicial hardening. By simply hiding the truth (i.e., that I was present and watching) I allowed my daughter to be tempted and to act in sin. Am I in any way culpable for that sin? No. I merely allowed it though I could have stopped it. Could God have stepped into the 1st century and clearly shown Himself in Christ to make all the Jews of that time believe Him? Of course. He could have ordained a "Damascus road experience" for every Jew if that was His will. It clearly was not.

Instead we see Christ telling His disciples to keep things quiet until the right time (Matt. 16:20). We see Him hiding the truth in parables (Mark 4:11). Why? If all people are born corpse-like dead, deaf, blind and unable to understand the truth, as Calvinism's doctrine of Total Inability suggests, why would Christ need to do this?

He did it because He knew revealing Himself could lead some to believe and He did not want them to come to repentance *yet* (not until after He is crucified and raised up does He draw all men to Himself, Jn. 12:32). This demonstrates that Jesus knew the truth was more than sufficient to draw the lost to repentance. He had a bigger redemptive purpose to accomplish through them first, so He "judicially hard-ened" them from seeing the otherwise enabling truth of God's Word.

Key Point: Do not allow the context of Israel's Judicial hardening cloud your view of mankind's inherent nature. People are very much capable of hearing, seeing and repenting when confronted by the powerful gospel truth if they have not yet "become calloused" to that truth (see Acts 28:27-28).

Non-Calvinists can and should affirm with our Calvinistic brethren that all men are born enemies of God (or at least born under the inevitable curse to become His enemy). Where we differ is in relation to the sufficiency of the gospel appeal sent by God Himself to invite all His enemies to be reconciled (2 Cor. 5:20). Is the "power of God unto Salvation" (Rom. 1:16) sufficient to enable those who hear it to respond willingly?

We can all agree that mankind is born sinful, but we disagree as to whether or not mankind is able to recognize and admit their sinfulness in light of God's clear and merciful revelation. We affirm with our Calvinistic brethren that all people are born enslaved, but we differ regarding whether or not the Holy Spirit wrought truth of God is sufficient to enable those in bondage to humbly admit they need help being freed from their chains. Indeed, we are born dead in rebellion, like the prodigal son in Jesus' parable (Lk. 15:32). But, we are never said to be "corpse-like" and thus unresponsive as was Lazarus in his tomb, an analogy never linked to soteriology by the Scripture despite what some Calvinists teach in their eisegetical reading of that narrative.[48]

---

[48] See John Piper's teaching titled: "Those Whom He Predestined He also Called." Web page: http://www.desiringgod.org/sermons/those-whom-he-predestined-he-also-called-part-1; [date accessed: 3/20/15].

Application

1) Joseph being sold by his brothers into slavery:

God's ultimate purpose, like that of the police officer in our analogy, is only good. The brother's intention, like that of the speeders, is not good. God's sovereign plan is to use their (libertarianly free) evil choices to accomplish His redemptive purpose, much like the officer's plan to accomplish his purpose through the free choice of speeders. God's intention is *only* to redeem, save, and restore throughout this entire event, yet to do so He must permit evil men to fulfill their own autonomously evil desires. There is no reason to suggest God determines the desires of the brothers any more so than there is to suggest the police officer determines the desires of the speeder. The Potter sinlessly used a sinful will to accomplish His promise.

2) Pharaoh hardened by God to accomplish the Passover:

Pharaoh libertarianly chose to rebel against God. God chose to blind Pharaoh from the truth so as to ensure he would remain in that rebellious condition until the redemptive purpose of the Passover was accomplished (a foreshadowing of Israel's hardening to accomplish the true Passover with Christ).

The text never suggests that God refused Pharaoh the ability to refrain or not refrain from his morally evil actions. Like the police officer hid his presence from the speeders, so too God hid His presence from Pharaoh. The Potter sinlessly used a sinful will to accomplish His promise.

3) The Crucifixion of Jesus:

Hendryx points people to God's determination of the crucifixion, "the worse evil of all time," to prove his perspective of meticulous providence. His argument goes something like this: *If God determined the worse evil of all time without blame then we should be able to accept that God can determine all evil events without blame.*

First, we should have no problem "blaming," or should I say "crediting," God with the redemption of sin as accomplished through the crucifixion. While I agree that God did determine the crucifixion by actively intervening in our fallen world to ensure it came to pass (by means of Judicial hardening as explained above), I fail to see how that proves God likewise determined and actively worked to bring about all the sin that needed redemption on that cross. Are we to believe God determined to redeem His very own determinations, or are we to believe the Potter sinlessly used a libertarianly sinful will to accomplish His redemptive promise?

Second, foreknowing that someone will libertarianly choose to sin, as I did with my daughter standing in front of the cookie jar, does not in any way imply such knowledge causes, determines or necessitates the desire of the sinner to sin. There is no reason we cannot merely accept that God is able to foreknow libertarianly free choices even though an element of mystery remains in the infinite nature of the One who knows. In short, I believe God knows the choices of His creatures because He is omniscient, not because He is "omni-deterministic."[49]

---

[49] "From God's knowledge that I shall do x, it does not follow that I must do x but only that I shall do x. That is in no way incompatible with my doing x freely. Undoubtedly, a major source of the fatalist's confusion is his conflating

Third, appealing to God's sovereign work to ensure the redemption of sin so as to prove that God sovereignly works to bring about all the sin that was redeemed is a self-defeating argument. It would be tantamount to arguing that because a police department
set up a sting operation to catch a notorious drug
dealer, that the police department is responsible for
every single intention and action of that drug dealer at
all times. Proof that the police department worked in
secretive ways to hide their identities, use evil intentions, and work out the circumstances in such a way
that the drug dealer would do what they wanted him
to do (sell drugs) at that particular moment in time
does not suggest that the police are in anyway responsible for all that drug dealer has done or ever will do.

We celebrate and reward the actions of this police
department because they are working to stop the drug
activity, not because they are secretly causing all of it
so as to stop some of it. Teaching that God brings
about all sin based on how He brought about Calvary
is like teaching that the police officer brings
about every drug deal based on how he brought
about one sting operation.

Understanding this doctrine prior to diving into
the teachings of Paul in Romans 9-11 is crucial. We
must have a clear view of the Potter's freedom in making choices so as to accomplish His redemptive promise.

Anticipated Objection:
You Sound Too Calvinistic

Despite my insistence that Judicial hardening is
for a good cause, even some of my non-Calvinistic

'certainty' with 'necessity.'" William Lane Craig, *Divine Foreknowledge: Four
Views* (p. 127). Kindle Edition.

friends have serious reservations about this teaching. And I admit, it is a fair concern. Should we really believe Jesus was intentionally obscuring the truth of His own identity while on earth? Does that teaching undermine God's goodness and love for all people? Can this perspective, like the Calvinistic one, be interpreted as violating human free will and moral responsibility?

Recently an esteemed mentor said to me, "It concerns me that you are conceding too much to the Calvinists on this point." He went on to tell me that phrases like "'Judicial hardening' are the kinds of phrases used by the Calvinist," implying we should avoid them. Though I have the deepest respect for this scholar, I simply disagree.

We cannot and should not attempt to avoid the clear biblical teaching of God's use of these Judicial means to accomplish His redemptive plan. After all, these issues are the ACTUAL objections being addressed in the controversial diatribe questions presented by Paul's interlocutor in Romans chapter 3 and chapter 9.

The doctrine of Judicial hardening (or similarly the "Messianic secret") should not be a troubling doctrine for any non-Calvinistic believer. In fact, when understood rightly, it highlights the gracious sovereignty of a God who loves and provides salvation for every man, woman, boy, and girl – yes, even calloused, self-righteous enemies of the gospel. (This point is fleshed out more thoroughly in chapter 6.)

Chapter 5

The Potter's Word

My research coming out of Calvinism brought three Bible passages into sharp focus: John 6, Ephesians 1 and Romans 8-9. These passages are the most referenced proof texts in support of TULIP doctrine.[50]

Many Calvinists cite John 6 to support their understanding of Total inability and Irresistible grace.[51] Additionally, much attention is directed toward Ephesians 1 to support the Calvinistic concept of the Unconditional election, understood as the predestination of individuals for regeneration.[52]

Calvinists also point to Rom. 8:28–9:33 to defend any objections brought against their doctrinal conclusions concerning Unconditional election, Limited atonement and Total inability.[53] Rom. 9:20 ("But who are you, a human being, to talk back to God?") is arguably the most quoted text by Calvinists in response to those who object to their views. Below is a critical analysis of these verses, with reference to other related passages in an effort to understand the whole counsel of Scripture concerning these soteriological matters.

---

[50] James R. White refers to these three passages, "Ephesians 1; Romans 9; John 6," as "the classicus locus" for the "exegetical defense of this divine truth" of Calvinism. Quote taken from: http://www.reformation-thelogy.com/2012/10/ ephesians_1_romans_9_john_6.php; [date accessed: 2/11/16].

Thomas Schreiner admits, "Calvinists typically appeal to Romans 9 to support their theology of divine election. In particular, they assert that Romans 9 teaches that God unconditionally elects individuals to be saved." Thomas R. Schreiner, "Does Romans 9 Teach Individual Election unto Salvation?" *in Still Sovereign: Contemporary Perspectives on Election, Foreknowledge, and Grace* (Grand Rapids: Baker, 2000), 89.

[51] David L. Allen and Steve W. Lemke, ed. *Whosoever Will: A Biblical-Theological Critique of Five-Point Calvinism* (Nashville: B&H Academic, 2010), 112–13.

[52] Ibid., 136–37.

[53] Ibid., 54, 119.

A Contextual Overview of John 6

Context provides the history, the setting, the audience and, thus, helps the reader understand the intention of the author. The grammar provides the interpretations which are allowed, but the author's intent is best discovered in the overall context. The historical narrative in which the sixth chapter of John was written provides significant understanding to the meaning of this largely contested chapter.

The audience in John 6 is a group of unbelieving Israelites looking for free food (vv. 25–31), and the twelve apostles (vs. 70).[54] Later in John's Gospel, Isaiah is quoted and this statement is explicitly identified with Jesus: "He has blinded their eyes and hardened their hearts, so they can neither see with their eyes, nor understand with their hearts, nor turn—and I would heal them."[55]

Jesus even wept over Israel because the truth was now being hidden from their eyes (Lk. 19:41-42). The Israelites were not born calloused, but over time their hearts were hardened in their religious self-righteousness, which led to the truth being hidden from them (see chapter 4). This, and only this, prevented the Jews of Christ's day from hearing, seeing, and responding to the revelation of God.

At this time the Israelites were being judicially hardened, or "cut off," (Rom. 9:1-3) and "sent a spirit of stupor" (Rom. 11:8) so as to seal them in their already-calloused condition (John 12:39–41; Acts 28:27). As seen throughout Scripture, God is hardening the calloused Jews in order to accomplish a greater

---

[54] Roger L. Fredrikson, *The Communicator's Commentary: John* (Waco, TX: Work Book Publishers, 1985), 130.

[55] John 12:40; cf. Isa. 6:10. John explicitly identifies Isaiah's statement with Jesus' glory in John 12:41.

redemptive purpose through their rebellion. God's ordained plan is to bring redemption to the world through the crucifixion of the Messiah by the hands of the rebellious Jews.

As previously discussed, Richard Soulen refers to Jesus's use of parabolic language (Matt. 13; Mark 4; John 6) and His warnings not to tell others that He was the Christ (Matt. 16:20; Mark 8:30) as the "Messianic secret." This addresses Jesus's expressed desire to keep His "messiah-ness" secret at times while here in the flesh.

Jesus provokes the Jewish religious leadership with very difficult teachings. In John 6:51–58, he tells them to eat His flesh and drink His blood without much explanation or clarification. Verses 60 and 61 clearly indicate the difficulty of these teachings for His audience. Jesus does not attempt to persuade this group to stay and support His teaching. Rather, He provokes them purposefully.[56]

Jesus addresses a group of people nicknamed the elect of God (i.e., Israelites) who have grown calloused toward His revelation. For that reason, they are blinded from recognizing the true identity of Jesus. This contextual information aids the expositor of John 6 attempting to understand the author's intention with regard to the natural abilities of mankind from birth, one of the primary points of contention between the Traditionalist and the Calvinist.

The judicially-hardened Jews are not the only ones present when Jesus was speaking in John 6. The twelve apostles are in the audience, and they are the

---

[56] Robert Gundry explains that not even Peter, or His closest followers, understood Jesus' messiah-ship as a suffering servant rather than the long expected conquering king. Robert H. Gundry, *A Survey of the New Testament, Revised Edition* (Grand Rapid, MI: Zondervan Publishing House, 1981), 148.

only ones who remained after Jesus finished provoking the crowd with His cannibalistic-toned, parabolic sermon (John 6:66–67).

The Twelve were not so offended as to leave behind their beloved teacher like the other followers. The Twelve were drawn to Him (John 6:44) through clear persuasive teachings and miraculous signs. They had been "taught of God" and had "learned from the Father" (John 6:45). Unlike the other Israelites in the audience, they watched Jesus walk on water, control the weather, heal the blind, feed the masses, and Jesus personally explained to them the meaning of the mysteries[57] that the world had not yet been given (Eph. 3:1-13).

Nothing is mentioned in the text of God using an inward, irresistible calling or work of regeneration to convince His apostles to remain faithful. Jesus had revealed His divine qualities through miraculous signs and wonders and explained His parabolic meanings to the Twelve many times before (Mark 4:11-34). They had already become well convinced of who Jesus was, as Peter indicated by saying, "We have come to believe and know that you are the Holy One of God" (John 6:69).

Jesus entrusted the truth to only a select few from Israel while He was "down from heaven" (John 6:38–42). The rest were being hardened in their already-calloused, self-righteous, stubborn condition. This was not their condition from birth due to Adam's sin, but a condition resulting from their own libertarianly free choices. God used this condition to accomplish a greater redemptive good for all.[58]

---

[57] Ibid, 148. Gundry wrote, "Jesus constantly sought privacy for the teaching of His disciples."

[58] See the discussion over the doctrine of Judicial hardening under the exegetical commentary of Rom. 9:19.

Calvinists often emphasize John 6:37 as it relates to verse 39 to argue the author intends to teach the notion that God has preselected a particular number of people to draw irresistibly while leaving all others without the ability to respond willingly to the revelation of God.[59] Consider, however, the contextual clue in verse 38, "For I have come down from heaven not to do my will but to do the will of Him who sent me." Here Jesus speaks about what is happening while He is "down from heaven."

While on earth, God sent Christ to accomplish a specific part of His redemptive will. That will was not to be a great evangelist and win thousands to faith, like Peter at Pentecost. Rather, God's will was for Jesus to come "down from heaven" and train a preselected group of Israelites (those given to Him to be apostles) to carry the gospel to the world and establish His church after He is raised from the dead (John 12:32; Matt. 28:19).

Some Calvinists fail to consider the first-century context and meaning of Jesus's words. Instead, they import the concept of the unconditional, effectual salvation of preselected individuals.[60] These same Calvinists fail to acknowledge the fact that Jesus, while "down from heaven," was judicially blinding Israel by means of riddles (Mark 4:11), a spirit of stupor (Rom. 11:8), and provoking language (John 6:60), while drawing to Himself a remnant of divinely-appointed

---

[59] In reference to this passage, John Calvin wrote, "What this statement amounts to is this: we should not be surprised if many people refuse to embrace the Gospel, since no one is ever able of himself to come to Christ unless God first comes to him by His Spirit. So it follows from this that not everyone is drawn, but that God gives this grace to those whom He has elected." Alister McGrath and J. I. Packer, ed. John Calvin, *The Crossway Classic Commentaries* (Wheaton: Crossway Books, 1994), 164.

[60] Fisher Humphreys and Paul Robertson observed, "The Calvinist reading of these verses is that God's drawing controls the response of the person..." Fisher Humphreys and Paul E. Robertson, *God So Loved The World: Traditional Baptists and Calvinism* (New Orleans: Insight Press, 2000), 73.

messengers from Israel. God selected the Jews to carry the Word of God to the nations (Isa. 49:6, Rom. 3:2, 9:5). The purpose from the beginning for which Israel had been elected was to bring the light to the rest of the world (Gen. 12:3).

The reason Jesus's audience in John 6 walked away was not because God rejected them before the foundation of the earth, as the Calvinistic rendering of this passage would suggest. Rather, God has consistently expressed His desire for the repentance and faith of every person (Matt. 23:37; Rom. 10:31; Ezek. 18:30–31; 2 Pet. 3:9; 1 Tim. 2:4; Hos. 3:1).

The audience walked away because God had sealed them in their rebellious condition for a period of time in order to accomplish His redemptive plan, as prophesied (Acts 2:23). Israel did not reject God because God rejected them. Rather, God temporarily hardened those in their rebellious, calloused condition in order to accomplish redemption for all,[61] including the very ones who were being judicially hardened (Rom. 11:14–23; 32). God's purpose in hardening Israel was redemptive, not retributive.

So, what is the intent of John 6? The Calvinistic systematic teaches that God decreed for all people to be born in a totally disabled condition due to the sin of Adam and has planned to irresistibly draw only a particular number of people for salvation, leaving the rest without any hope of responding to His appeals for reconciliation.[62] The non-Calvinist teaches that Jesus was

---

[61] Luke Johnson speaks of the Jewish leader's inability to recognize Jesus as their messiah because the truth is "hidden from them." Luke Timothy Johnson, *The Writings of the New Testament* (Philadelphia: Fortress Press, 1986), 484.

[62] John Calvin taught, "All are not created on equal terms, but some are preordained to eternal life, others to eternal damnation; and, accordingly, as each has been created for one or other of those ends, we say that he has been predestined to life or death." John Calvin, *Institutes of the Christian Religion*, trans. Henry Beveridge (Grand Rapids: Christian Classics Ethereal Library, 2002), Sec. 5, 1030–31.

provoking Israel in their hardened unbelief, while also drawing a remnant of divinely-appointed messengers to take the gospel to the world so as to draw all to Himself after he was raised up. As Jesus explained, "And I, when I am lifted up from the earth, will draw all people to myself" (John 12:32).

An Overview of Ephesians 1

Ephesians 1 is another contested passage regarding the doctrine of salvation. The first verse indicates that Paul's audience was "the faithful in Christ Jesus." In fact, the "in Christ" theme introduced in the apostle's opening sentence continues through this entire section of the text. He repeated this phrase, in various forms, ten times in thirteen verses.[63]

The Calvinist contends that certain individuals were chosen before the world began and predestined to become believers,[64] but that is simply not what the text says. Paul teaches that those "in Him" have been predestined to become "holy and blameless" and "to be adopted as sons," but he never says that certain individuals were predestined to believe in Christ. Paul speaks of what "the faithful in Christ" (vs. 1) have been predestined to become, not about God preselecting certain individuals before the foundation of the world to be irresistibly transformed into believers.

Whosoever believes in Him is predestined to become "holy and blameless in His sight," (vs. 4) which parallels Paul's teaching in Rom. 8:29, which says, "he also predestined (those who love God, Rom. 8:28) to

---

[63] "The phrase 'in Christ,' which occurs 164 times in the Pauline literature of the N. T., can be called the key to Pauline theology." George Arthur Buttrick, ed. *The Interpreter's Bible, Vol. 10*. (Nashville: Abingdon Press, 1953), 612.

[64] R. C. Sproul, *Chosen by God* (Wheaton, IL: Tyndale House, 1986), 136-158.

be conformed to the imagine of His Son." Paul is referring to the sanctification of all who come to be *in Him*
through faith. Every believer, regardless of their nationality, will be "conformed to the image of Christ" by
being made "holy and blameless." How can one be so
certain? God has predestined it. This is why Paul refers
to a "guarantee" in verse 14 of the same chapter.

Paul continues to speak of what the believer is to
chosen to become when he writes, "He predestined us
("the faithful in Christ") for adoption to sonship
through Jesus Christ," (vs. 5). According to Paul, believers "wait eagerly for our adoption to sonship, the
redemption of our bodies" (Rom. 8:23), because that
is what believers have been predestined to become.
Believers are not fully adopted until they take up resi-
dence in the home of the one who has adopted them.
Until that point, they look forward with great anticipa-
tion to their "adoption," for which they have been predestined.

Does Paul ever state that God chose individuals to
be effectually placed in Him, or does it simply state, he
chose those who are in Him? Does the Scripture teach
that Christ redeems individuals so that they might irresistibly be placed in Him, or does it only teach that
believers in Him have redemption? Did Paul ever actually say that God has chosen particular individuals
to be effectually placed in Him, or does it simply say
that "believers in Him were also chosen?"

If we continually remind ourselves that the "us"
being referenced through this chapter are "the faithful
in Christ" (vs. 1), then the apostle's intention becomes
quite clear. Before the foundation of the world God has
predestined us, the faithful in Christ, to become holy
and to be adopted (vs. 4-5).

The main point of contention between Traditionalists and Calvinists is how one comes to be in Him.
Some focus so much attention on the first twelve

verses that they fail to see the following two verses where Paul gives an answer to this vital question.[65] Paul states in verse 13a, "And you also were included in Christ *when you heard the message of truth, the gospel of your salvation*" (emphasis mine).

Were individuals included in Christ before the foundation of the earth? No, Paul wrote it was "when you heard the message of truth, the gospel of your salvation." He continues, "*When you believed*, you were marked in Him..." (emphasis mine). Were these believers marked in Him before the world began and without regard to their response to the gospel? No, Paul states clearly that individuals were marked "in Him" *when they believed* the message of truth.[66]

Paul indicates that God has predestined for "the faithful in Christ Jesus" (vs. 1) to become "holy and blameless" (vs. 4) and to be "adopted" (vs. 5).[67] Believers in Christ can know they will be sanctified and glorified because God has marked them "in Him" and given them His Spirit as a guarantee of what He has purposed for all who believe.

The first chapter of Ephesians is not about God predetermining which individuals will be in Christ. This passage is about God predetermining the spiritual blessings for those who are in Christ through believing the word of truth (vv. 1-3).

---

[65] When he speaks of 'we' and 'us' in the preceding verses, the writer clearly includes all Christian believers. Here (in verses 11-12), however, the first person applies only to the people of Israel, with whom he identifies with himself, in distinction from the Gentile believers (you also) to whom he turns in vs. 13. Herschel Hobbs, Study in Ephesians: *New Men in Christ* (Waco, TX: Word Book, 1974), 24.

[66] Herschel Hobbs wrote, "God in His sovereignty marked out beforehand the boundaries of 'in Christ,' and elected that all who are in Christ shall be saved. Men in their free will chose to be 'in Christ' by faith or to be outside of Christ in refusal to believe in Him as Savior." Ibid. 25.

[67] Romans 8:23 indicates Paul sees adoption as a future hope for all who come to God through faith. Romans 8:29 teaches that being conformed to Christ's image, like being made "holy and blameless," is also a predetermined plan for all who love God (vs. 28).

God has invited all to come to Christ and enter into His rest (Matt. 28:19; 11:28; Mark 16:15; John 12:32; 2 Cor. 5:19–21; Col. 1:23), and He genuinely desires all to come (2 Pet. 3:9; 1 Tim. 2:4; Ezek. 18:30–32; Matt. 23:37; Rom. 10:21). All who come will be trained (sanctified, conformed to His image, Rom. 8:29) and guaranteed a place (adopted, glorified, Rom. 8:23), because that is what God has predetermined for all who are *in Him.*

Prior to Christ's coming, Israel was commonly understood to be *the elect of God.* The nation as a whole, and thus individuals from within that nation, were the chosen people through which the good news would be brought to the rest of the world (Rom. 3:2). However, the people of Israel were "bound up in the problem instead of being the bringers of the solution," says N.T. Wright.[68] Therefore, if salvation for the world was to be accomplished, it would come to pass through different means.

Jesus Christ came as the solution to this very dilemma. The grand narrative continues with the Messiah accomplishing "for the world what Israel was called to do."[69] Israel is not the only elect means through which salvation's hope is delivered. Jesus is the elect One (Mt. 12:18). Election is redefined with Christ as the central figure, which is why many Israelites of Paul's day fought so vehemently against His teachings. As Markus Barth wrote, "God administers and carries out election through Jesus Christ."[70] Ralph Martin similarly states, "Election is . . . universalized

---

[68] N. T. Wright, *Paul: In Fresh Perspective* (Minneapolis: Fortress press, 2005), 119.

[69] Ibid., 120.

[70] Markus Barth, *Ephesians 1–3, The Anchor Bible, Vol. 34,* eds. William Foxwell Albright and David Noel Freedman (Garden City: Doubleday, 1974), 107.

to include all who are in Christ."[71] Since Christ is the elect One, "those who hear the gospel and respond to it in faith are then declared to be [God's] people, His elect."[72]

Study of Romans 8:28–9:33

Due to the overwhelming popularity of this passage when it comes to the defense of Calvinistic soteriology, I feel it is necessary to provide a verse by verse exegetical commentary from a traditional non-Calvinistic perspective.

Romans 8:28

And we know that in all things God works for the good of those who love Him, who have been called according to His purpose.

The Greek verb *oida* ("we know") is a perfect active indicative form of the verb, which may simply refer to knowledge gained by observance or remembrance of the past. This is paralleled earlier in verse 22 (using the same Greek verb tense of *oida*) when speaking about their observation of creation "groaning as in the pains of childbirth right up to the present time."

Paul seems to be saying "we have observed" and "therefore we know." The context and grammar appear to indicate a reference not to an intuitive knowledge of Paul's readers, but to that which comes from observation of the past, or a remembrance.[73]

Paul means that believers know, from observation of God's past dealings with those who love Him, that

---

[71] Ralph P. Martin, *Ephesians, Colossians, and Philemon*, ed. James Luther Mays (Louisville: John Knox Press, 1991), 18.

[72] Wright, *Paul: In Fresh Perspective*, 122.

[73] Johannes P. Louw and Eugene A. Nida, *Lexicon of the New Testament: Based on Semantic Domains, Second Edition* (New York: United Bible Societies, 1989), 29.6.

he has a mysterious way of working things out for the greatest good. By observing the stories of the saints of old—those called to accomplish His redemptive purposes—believers can rest in knowledge of this truth. God can take whatever evil may come our way and redeem it for good. Believers can know this because God has been doing it for generations.

Paul does not say that his readers should intuitively know how God works things out for those who love Him in the present. He is saying believers know what is true of God by observing what He has done in the past for those who have loved Him. The New Testament saints have a great cloud of witnesses that have gone before them (Heb. 12:1), giving evidence of God's trustworthiness toward all who enter into a covenant with Him.

A simple survey of the verses leading up to this point reveals that Paul is reflecting on the problem of the evil and suffering in our world since the beginning:

Rom. 8:20-22: "For the creation was subjected to futility, not willingly, but because of Him who subjected it, in hope that the creation itself also will be set free from its slavery to corruption into the freedom of the glory of the children of God. For we know that the whole creation groans and suffers the pains of childbirth together until now."

N. T. Wright comments on Rom. 8:28–30, saying in part:

"[This passage] is a sharp, close-up, compressed telling of the story of Israel, as the chosen people, whose identity and destiny is then brought into sharp focus on Jesus. Jesus, in a sense, is the one 'chosen One.' But, then that identity is shared with all of those who are 'in Christ.' And he [Paul] is not talking primarily there about salvation. He is talking primarily about the way God is healing the whole creation. There is a danger here. What has happened in so many theological circles over the years is that people have come to the text assuming that it is really saying how we are to get to heaven, and what is the mechanism and how does that work. And if you do that, interestingly, many exegetes will more or less skip over Romans 8:18–27, which is about the renewing of creation."[74]

In verses 28 and 29 the focus shifts to providing comfort for those in suffering by reminding them to observe God's dealings with others who loved God throughout history. Notice that this truth is not applicable to everyone. The passage is specifically an observation of those who "love God," or as Wright notes, "those who are in Christ."

The point is not that God causes everything for a good purpose, but that God redeems occurrences of evil for a good purpose in the lives of those who love Him. Therefore, it would be inaccurate to use this passage to support the concept of divine meticulous determinism of all things.[75] Again, God does not cause occurrences of evil for His purposes; instead, He redeems moral evil for a good purpose. Traditionalists would typically agree with what John MacArthur, a Calvinistic pastor, wrote on this point:

"But God's role with regard to evil is never as its author. He simply permits evil agents to work, then overrules evil for His own wise and holy

---

[74] N. T. Wright in a question and answer session at Oklahoma Christian University on April 1, 2014. Samuel Selvin, "Dr. N. T. Wright on predestination," YouTube video, 05:08, https://www.youtube.com/watch-?v=qK-wIijhZW-M; [date accessed: 10/10/15].

[75] This is also true of Eph. 1:11, which is often misapplied to support the idea of meticulous determinism.

ends. Ultimately He is able to make all things—
including all the fruits of all the evil of all time—
work together for a greater good."[76]

The focus of the apostle's observation is on the
saints of old, those from the elect nation of Israel who
were called to fulfill God's plan to redeem His creation
from its groans and sufferings. This passage does not
mean that the truth being revealed is not applicable to
those of other nations. Rather, it means that what is
proven to be true of God by observing His dealings
with those called out from Israel throughout history
must also be true of anyone who comes to follow and
love the God of Israel.

Consider this analogy: Suppose a new pastor is
called to a church. The staff members are nervous
about his leadership style and how they might be
treated, but a letter of reference which reflects on his
past relationships might ease their fears. The pastor's
reference might say something like, *I have observed
this pastor's dealings with the staff members he knew
before, and he has always worked to lovingly support
anyone who gets behind the vision and direction of
the church.* By reflecting on the pastor's history, the
new staff can know what to expect in their future dealings with him. So too, Paul gives a divine reference by
reflecting on the trustworthiness of God in His dealings with the saints of old so as to ensure his readers
of what they may expect of Him.

Romans 8:29
**For those God foreknew He also predes-
tined to be conformed to the image of His**

---

[76] John MacArthur, "Is God Responsible for Evil?" Grace To You Ministries web page. Quote taken from: http://www.gty.org/ resources /arti-
cles/A189/is-god-responsible-for-evil; [date accessed: 5/19/15].

Son, that He might be the firstborn among many brothers and sisters.

Here the apostle reveals his focus on the saints of old, "those God foreknew." Paul seeks to provide evidence of his claim in verse 28 by reflecting on God's faithfulness to His chosen nation, those beloved who were known before. Paul provides a reference of sorts to ease the fears of those who are now coming to faith. This point continues to be the apostle's focus for the next three chapters.

Much debate centers on the meaning of the word *proginōskō* ("to know beforehand").[77] Many popular authors fail to recognize all the available options for consideration. For example, John Piper lists only two options for interpreting this verse:

Option #1: God foresaw our self-determined faith. We remain the decisive cause of our salvation. God responds to our decision to believe.

Option #2: God chose us—not on the basis of foreseen faith, but on the basis of nothing in us. He called us, and the call itself creates the faith for which it calls.[78]

Piper overlooks the most basic meaning of this word, which is "to know beforehand" or to have known in the past. The same Greek word is used by Peter and Paul in the following passages,

2 Pet. 3:17: "Therefore, dear friends, since you have been *forewarned,* be on your guard so that

---

[77] The definition of *proginōskō* is from *The Lexham Analytical Lexicon to the Greek New Testament* (Bellingham, WA: Logos Bible Software, 2011), 30.100.

[78] John Piper, Sermon: "Foreknown by God," Quote taken from: http://www.desiringgod.org/labs/foreknown-by-god; [date accessed: 10/19/16].

you may not be carried away by the error of the lawless and fall from your secure position."

Acts 26:4–5: "The Jewish people all know the way I have lived ever since I was a child, from the beginning of my life in my own country, and also in Jerusalem. *They have known* me for a long time and can testify, if they are willing, that I conformed to the strictest sect of our religion, living as a Pharisee."

Clearly, this word can be understood simply as knowing someone or something in the past, as in those known previously (i.e., the saints of old). Non-Calvinistic scholars, Roger Forster and Paul Marston, convincingly argue,

"God 'foreknew them' or 'knew them of old' thus it does not mean that God entered in some former time into a relationship with the Israelites of today, it means that he entered a (two-way) relationship with the Israel that existed in early Old Testament times, and he regards the present Israelites as integral with it."[79]

If Paul intended to use the word *proginōskō* in this sense, then he meant simply that because we have seen how God worked all things to the good for those whom *He knew before*, we know that He will do the same for those who love and are called by Him now.

Some Calvinists contend that the word foreknew is equivalent to fore-loved. That use of the word generally fits this interpretation since the Israelites of the past who loved God certainly would have been loved

---

[79] Roger T. Forster and V. Paul Marston, *God's Strategy in Human History* (Wheaton: Tyndale, 1973), 179–90.

by God before (i.e., fore-loved). Of course, the Calvin-istic interpretation differs because they insist this pas-sage is about God unconditionally setting His "effec-tual" salvific love upon certain individuals before the foundation of the world. Calvinists go to great lengths to show that God did not merely foresee the behavior and choices of the elect by looking down the corridors of time. Rather, God knew them intimately and set His effectual love on them before the foundation of the world.[80]

This argument might address the classical Armin-ian approach (Piper's first option),[81] but it fails to re-but the approach being advocated here. Fore-loved is a viable and even likely meaning of the term *proginōskō*, yet it does not clarify who might be the intended target of that divine love.

Was Paul intending to introduce for the first time in this epistle a particular group of people out of the mass of humanity who were unconditionally elected to be effectually saved before the world began? Or, was he simply referencing those from the past whom God had known and faithfully cared for throughout the generations?

Romans 8:29b states "He (God) also predestined to become conformed to the image of His Son." Who was "predestined" and to what ends were they predes-tined, according to this passage? Remember the point of the apostle leading up to this verse. He began speak-ing about the futility and suffering that has come into

---

[80] John Murray, *The Epistle to the Romans, Volume I* (Grand Rapids, MI: Eerdmans Publishing, 1959), 316-318.

[81] Frederic Godet's commentary on Romans 8:29 inquires: "In what re-spect did God thus foreknow them?" and answers that they were "foreknown as sure to fulfill the conditions of salvation, viz. faith; so: foreknown as His by faith." The word "foreknew" is thus understood by Godet, a classical Arminian, to mean that God knew beforehand which sinners would believe, and on the basis of this knowledge He predestined them unto salvation. Frederic Godet, *Commentary on the Epistle to the Romans* (New York: Messrs Clark, 1880), 325.

this world due to the fall of humanity into sin (vv. 20–22). In verse 28-29a, Paul provides comfort to lovers of God in his audience by reminding them of God's trustworthiness for those who have loved Him throughout the generations.

Paul reminds his readers that God will redeem the suffering and evil for a good purpose in their lives just as he has done in the lives of those *known before* and loved throughout the previous generations. It is these whom God *previously knew* (Israelites whom loved God in the past) who were predestined to be conformed into the image of Christ so as to make the way for His coming.

God planned to accomplish salvation for those who were *previously known* and loved (i.e., Abraham, Moses, David, etc.) by conforming them into the image of the One who would come to purchase their redemption. This is the ultimate example of God causing "all things to work for the good" of those saints of old who loved God. Paul is saying that God brings about the redemption of their souls and He will do the same for whoever loves Him. N. T. Wright states,

> "Here is the note of hope which has been sounded by implication so often since it was introduced in 5:2: hope for the renewal of all creation, in a great act of liberation for which the exodus from Egypt was simply an early type. As a result, all that Israel hoped for, all that it based its hope on, is true of those who are in Christ."[82]

---

[82] N. T. Wright, *Pauline Theology, Volume III*, ed. David M. Hay & E. Elizabeth Johnson (Minneapolis: Fortress, 1995), 30–67, Quote taken from: http://ntwrightpage.com/Wright_Romans_Theology_Paul.pdf. [date accessed 9/7/15].

Romans 8:29c states "that He (the Son) might be the firstborn among many brothers and sisters." Consider the fact that he is speaking about what Christ *might be*, which strongly implies that Paul still has the saints of old in focus here. Why would Paul speak of future generations being conformed to the image of Christ so that He "*might be* the firstborn among many brothers and sisters" if He were already the firstborn prior to this discourse?

The term *prōtotokos* ("firstborn") can simply refer to the one who is first to be born in a family, which carries much significance in the Jewish culture (Luke 2:7). Typically, the birthright given to the firstborn son signified a place of preeminence, by which he would receive the father's inheritance and blessing. For instance, Psalm 89:20, 27 states, "I have found David my servant; with my sacred oil I have anointed him. . . And I will appoint him to be my firstborn, the most exalted of the kings of the earth." David, who was the last one born in his family, was called by God the firstborn. David was given a place of preeminence.[83]

The term firstborn also speaks of Christ's preexistence as the eternal Creator.[84] God created the world through Christ and redeemed the world through Christ (John 1:3, 10; Heb. 1:2–4). The former speaks of His eternal nature and the latter of His temporal role as the redeemer of the world.

Yet, even when speaking of our preexistent Lord, the biblical authors addressed Him as "becoming" or "fulfilling" His role as our Messiah within the temporal

---

[83] James D. G. Dunn, *Romans 1-8, Word Biblical Commentary,* ed. David A. Hubbard and Glenn W. Barker, Vol. 38a (Dallas: Word, 1988), 1: 484.

[84] Theologian Bernard Ramm noted that "It has been standard teaching in historic Christology that the Logos, the Son, existed before the incarnation. That the Son so existed before the incarnation has been called the pre-existence of Christ." Bernard Ramm, *An Evangelical Christology: Ecumenic and Historic* (Vancouver, BC: Regent College Publishing, 1993) 47.

world. For example, the Psalmist writes, "And I will appoint Him to be my firstborn, the most exalted of the kings of the earth" (Ps. 89:27). For the Old Testament saints, the firstborn Savior was the expected One that was yet to come. From their view, the long-awaited Messiah was the future hope, not a past and completed reality.

In contrast to the Old Testament saints, a modern-day preacher would not teach that we are being conformed to Christ's image so that Jesus *might be* the firstborn among many brethren, because we know Him to already be the firstborn of many brethren. Our being conformed into Christ's image today has nothing to do with the future coming of Christ's birth, whereas the saints of old were part of His very lineage. It is through the life of men like Abraham, Isaac, Jacob, David, and many other saints of old that Christ is brought into this world "that He *might be* the firstborn among many brothers and sisters (Rom. 8:29c)."

Paul is reflecting on God's redemptive purpose being accomplished through those who loved God in former generations. That redemptive purpose included bringing the Messiah into this world through Israel (Rom. 9:4-5), or those Israelites set apart for that noble purpose (Rom. 9:21). This was God's pre-destined plan of redemption, which was brought to pass through those who loved God and were called according to His purpose. Tim Warner describes this purpose,

> "Paul was not referring to some prior knowledge in the mind of God before creation. Nor was He speaking about predetermining their fate. He was referring to those whom God knew personally and intimately, men like Abraham and David.

The term 'foreknew' does not mean to have knowledge of someone before they were conceived. The verb προεγνω is the word for 'know' (in an intimate sense) with the preposition προ (before) prefixed to it. It refers to having an intimate relationship with someone in the past... Literally, we could render Rom. 8:29 as follows: 'For those God formerly knew intimately, He previously determined them to be conformed to the image of His Son.'

The individual saints of old, with whom God had a personal relationship, were predestined by Him to be conformed to the image of Christ. That is, God predetermined to bring their salvation to completion by the sacrifice of Christ on their behalf." [85]

Likewise, William R. Newell, a colleague of D.L. Moody and a notable teacher at the Bible Moody College, explained that God "had acquaintanceship" with the Israelites of the past. So, it was not "mere Divine pre-knowledge" of certain individuals, but a real intimate "pre-acquaintanceship."[86]

Romans 8:30
And those He predestined, He also called; those He called, He also justified; those He justified, He also glorified.

---

[85] Tim Warner, *PFRS Commentary on Romans*, Pristine Faith Restoration Society. Quote taken from: http://www.pfrs.org/commentary/Rom_8-_28.pdf; [date accessed: 10/15/15].

[86] William R. Newell, *"Romans Verse-by-Verse," Christian Classics Ethereal Library*, 1938. Quote taken from: https://play.google.com/books/-reader?id=CWhyfIWOg8C&printsec=frontcover&ouput=reader&hl=en&pg=GBS.PP1; [date accessed: 4/9/16].

Notice the apostle's use of the past tense in this verse. If Paul intended to speak about the future salvation of every elect individual, then why would he use these past tense verbs? When writing these words, Paul and his readers had not yet been glorified, so there is no explicit reason to use the past tense. Thus, there is no reason to assume Paul has in mind the future glorification of all believers.

The past tense suggests that Paul is referring to former generations of those who have loved God and were called to fulfill His redemptive purpose. They were known in the past generations and predestined by God to be made in the very image of the One to come, "the firstborn among many brothers and sisters," which is something already completed in the past through the working of God in former generations. These are the individuals whom God called, justified, and who now, even as Paul was writing these words, are already glorified in the presence of God.

If indeed Paul was referencing the saints formerly known and loved by God, he would have communicated the certainty of their being justified, sanctified and finally glorified in a way that some might describe as a "golden chain of redemption."[87] To presume, however, that Paul's unbroken chain of past tense verbs is not in reference to people of the past is a linguistic stretch. [88]

Calvinists must explain away the use of the past tense verbs in order to maintain their interpretation of Paul's intent. For instance, *The Bible Knowledge*

---

[87] Some Calvinistic scholars describe this as the unbreakable "golden chain of redemption" meant to communicate the unchangeable plan of God to irrevocably justify, sanctify and glorify those He elected before the world began.

[88] Greek scholars teach that while the aorist indicative can be used to describe an event that is not yet past as though it were already completed, this usage is "not at all common." Daniel B. Wallace, *Greek Grammar Beyond the Basics* (Grand Rapids, MI: Zondervan Publishing, 1997) 564.

Commentary, a Calvinistic source, provides this explanation, "Glorified is in the past tense because this final step is so certain that in God's eyes it is as good as done."[89]

Calvinists must interpret Paul's use of the past tense (aorist indicative) as meaning "it is as good as done" because it was predestined. But this is a very rare usage in the original language and the immediate context does not clearly support a Calvinistic rendering.

We must take into account Paul's usage of the same term earlier in the chapter as a future hope for believers.

Romans 8:17: "Now if we are children, then we are heirs—heirs of God and co-heirs with Christ, *if indeed we share in His sufferings in order that we may also share in His glory"* (emphasis added).

Paul does not speak of glorification as a past and completed action in reference to the believers in his day. Rather, he seems to qualify their being glorified upon the condition that they persevere through the suffering that is to come. If it is "as good as done" due to God's predetermination, then why would Paul make such a qualification and use the future tense of the same verb? Further, Paul speaks of the eager expectation of the glorification that is to come in verses 22–25:

---

[89] John F. Walvoord and Roy B. Zuck, eds. *The Bible Knowledge Commentary* (Dallas: Victor Books, 1983), 474.

"And all this is viewed as past; because, starting from the past decree of 'predestination to be conformed to the image of God's Son' of which the other steps are but the successive unfoldings—all is beheld as one entire, eternally completed salvation." Jamieson-Fausset-Brown Bible Commentary, "Romans 8." Quote take from: http://biblehub.com/commentaries/jfb/romans /8.htm; [date accessed: 10/22/15].

"We know that the whole creation has been groaning as in the pains of childbirth right up to the present time. Not only so, but we ourselves, who have the firstfruits of the Spirit, groan inwardly as *we wait eagerly for our adoption to sonship, the redemption of our bodies.* For in this hope we were saved. But hope that is seen is no hope at all. Who hopes for what they already have? But if we hope for what we do not yet have, we wait for it patiently" (emphasis added).

Is the reader to believe that Paul shifts from speaking of glorification as a future hope for those who persevere, to speaking of it as a past and already-completed act for those who have not yet been glorified? Or, could it simply be that Paul has the Old Testament saints in view as he makes his case for the trustworthiness of God throughout all generations? The latter seems to be the most basic understanding of the apostle's words in their context.

This interpretation may seem foreign to some Western readers because of the philosophical and theological baggage that has been attached to the concept of divine foreknowledge over the years, but to the first century reader the simple concept of *proginōskō*, understood as "previously known," would have been far more likely. In fact, if one can objectively back away from their presuppositions and approach this passage with fresh eyes, I believe they will discover the utter simplicity and clarity of this perspective.

Instead of introducing a complex concept of divine prescience, unconditional election, and effectual salvation never once clearly expounded upon in the Scriptures, could it be that Paul may intend simply to communicate that those who were previously loved

and known by God were also predestined to be conformed to the image of the One to come? Paul seems
to be giving a brief history lesson of what God had
done in former generations as a reference for God's
trustworthiness for all who come to Him in faith.
Wright explains it this way:

> "The creation is not god, but it is designed to be
> flooded with God: The Spirit will liberate the
> whole creation. Underneath all this, of course, re-
> mains Christology: the purpose was that the Mes-
> siah 'might be the firstborn among many siblings'
> (8.29). Paul is careful not to say, or imply, that the
> privileges of Israel are simply 'transferred to the
> church,' even though, for him, the church means
> Jews-and-gentiles-together in Christ. Rather, the
> destiny of Israel has devolved, entirely appropri-
> ately within the Jewish scheme, upon the Mes-
> siah. All that the new family inherit, they inherit
> in Him."[90]

Those who object to the suggestion that Paul's use
of the term *proginōskō* is limited to the beloved of Israel's past should consider the apostle's use of the
same word just three chapters later,

> **Rom. 10:21-11:2a:** "But concerning Israel he
> says, 'All day long I have held out my hands to a
> disobedient and obstinate people.' I ask then: Did
> God reject His people? By no means! I am an Is-
> raelite myself, a descendant of Abraham, from the
> tribe of Benjamin. God did not reject His peo-
> ple, whom he *foreknew*" (emphasis added).

---

90 Wright, *Pauline Theology*, 20.

Notice that Paul uses the term *proginōskō* in reference to God's intimate relationship with the faithful Israelites of old. Paul continues to make his case,

> **Rom. 11:2b-4**: "Don't you know what Scripture says in the passage about Elijah—how he appealed to God against Israel: 'Lord, they have killed your prophets and torn down your altars; I am the only one left, and they are trying to kill me?' And what was God's answer to him? 'I have reserved for myself seven thousand who have not bowed the knee to Baal.'"

Elijah and those who refused to bow a knee were among the ones who were *previously known* (foreknown/fore-loved) by God. *To foreknow* refers to God's intimate relationship with people who loved Him in the past (like Abraham in Rom. 4:22–5:5). Nothing in this or any other text supports the concept of God in eternity past preselecting certain individuals out of the mass of humanity for effectual salvation. It would be difficult to substantiate this meaning of the term *foreknow* in reference to the Israelites who were in covenant with God. It is best interpreted in reference to those known by God in former times. William Lane Craig explains,

> "In certain cases, *proginōskō* and *prooraō* mean simply that one has known or seen (someone or something) previously. For example, in Acts 26:5 Paul states that the Jews had previously known for a long time the strictness of his life as a Pharisee, and in Acts 21:29 Luke mentions that the Jews had previously seen (*prooraō*) Trophimus in Paul's company. This sense is probably operative in Romans 11:2 as well, where Paul states of apostate Israel that 'God has not rejected His people

whom He foreknew [*proginōskō*],' that is, whom He had previously known in an intimate way."[91]

Romans 8:31–39

Returning to the analogy above, the pastor had former staff members whom he intimately knew and loved. The new staff would be comforted to know of the pastor's prior relationships. Likewise, those being grafted into covenant with the God of Israel for the first time (i.e., the Gentiles) would be thrilled to learn of God's faithfulness to those He formerly knew and loved (i.e., men like Abraham and David, etc.). What can the readers say in response to these teachings of Paul about God's faithfulness toward the saints of old?

That is the very question the apostle poses in Rom. 8:31a as he transitions to the application of His message,

"What, then, shall we say in response to these things?"

This interpretation is consistent with the view that present-day saints who love God and are called according to His purposes (vs. 28) have nothing to fear, for...

"If God is for us, who can be against us?" (vs. 31b).

God, who gave up His Son, justifies, intercedes, and places His undying love upon all who love Him and are called according to His purposes (vv. 32–39).

The objector in Paul's mind asks: *Paul, you have made a good case regarding God's faithfulness to the*

---

[91] William Lane Craig, *The Only Wise God: The Compatibility of Divine Foreknowledge and Human Freedom* (Grand Rapids: Baker, 1987), 31–32.

*Israelites in the past, but what about the Israelites to-
day? Have God's promises for Israel failed? Why are
the Israelites today refusing to accept their own Messiah?* The apostle attempts to answer these questions
in Romans 9 and following.

Romans 9:1–4a

**I speak the truth in Christ—I am not ly-
ing, my conscience confirms it through the
Holy Spirit—I have great sorrow and un-
ceasing anguish in my heart. For I could
wish that I myself were cursed and cut off
from Christ for the sake of my people, those of my own race the people of Israel.**

Paul, modeling the very nature of his self-sacrificial Savior, begins this chapter with a heartfelt, an-
guished plea for the souls of his fellow kinsmen. Despite the fact that they have become his enemies, the
apostle follows the example of Christ by sincerely loving them with a sacrificial passion that could only
come from the Spirit Himself (Matt. 5:43-48). As with
Jesus, this love was demonstrated in word and deed.
Paul expresses the nature of Christ by his willingness
to take the wrath due to his fellow countrymen.

The apostle emphasizes the fact that his feelings
are in full agreement with that of the Holy Spirit Himself, as distinguished from his own limited human
emotion or opinion, as some may attempt to suggest
(1 Cor. 7:12). This divine pleading, patience, and long-
suffering toward the nation of Israel is reflected in this
context and throughout all of Scripture (Hos. 3:1;
Rom. 9:22, 10:1, 21, 11:1, 11–14; Matt. 23:37; Luke
19:41–42). Paul begins and ends Romans 10 by expressing this same affection,

Rom. 10:1, 21: "Brothers and sisters, my heart's desire and prayer to God for the Israelites is that they may be saved...But concerning Israel He says, 'All day long I have held out my hands to a disobedient and obstinate people.'"

Despite Paul's explicit desire to perish in the place of these hardened Jews, five-point Calvinists teach that Christ does not share Paul's expressed intentions.[92] One has to assume that those interpreters believe Paul was more merciful and self-sacrificial than the Savior who inspired these very words. It is inexplicable, given Paul's Spirit-led appeal of self-sacrificial love, to promote a doctrine that teaches Jesus did not intend to sacrifice Himself for these hardened Jews (1 John 2:2; 2 Pet. 2:1).

Romans 9:4b–5

Theirs is the adoption to sonship; theirs the divine glory, the covenants, the receiving of the law, the temple worship and the promises. Theirs are the patriarchs, and from them is traced the human ancestry of the Messiah, who is God over all, forever praised! Amen.

The apostle continues with the objection introduced and answered in Romans 2–3, What advantage has the Jew? Or what is the benefit of circumcision, since salvation is for all nations? He answers, "Great in every respect. First of all, the Jews were entrusted with the words of God" (Rom. 3:1-2). Paul explains,

---

92 Some Calvinists are "four pointers" (Amyraldians). They deny limited atonement, the view that Christ only gave His life for those unconditionally elected before the foundation of the world rather than for every person. As an example, see James White, "*Was Anyone Saved at the Cross?*" Web page, available from http://vintage.aomin.org/ Was%20Anyone% 20Saved.html; [date accessed: 3/24/15].

Rom. 2:28-29: "For he is not a Jew who is one outwardly, nor is circumcision that which is outward in the flesh. But he is a Jew who is one inwardly; and circumcision is that which is of the heart, by the Spirit, not by the letter; and his praise is not from men, but from God."

Two major points of the apostle in Romans 2–3 are clear. First, salvation is intended for whoever believes, regardless of their nationality. Second, a blessing or benefit still exists for being of ethnic Israel.[93] For example, "the Jews have been entrusted with the very words of God" (Rom. 3:2).

In Romans 9, Paul develops these two points in light of the fact that so many Israelites do not believe the very words that have been entrusted to them. By showing that not every Israelite from the seed of Abraham is chosen for the noble purpose of carrying the Word of God, Paul seeks to prove that God's promise to Abraham has not failed, that "all peoples on earth will be blessed through you" (Gen. 12:3b).

Paul's reference to Israel carries significance. Some linguistic scholars point to the root meaning of this new name given to Jacob as relating to the primitive root verb שרה, which refers to the authority of a prince.[94] The ultimate authority is reserved for the king, but the prince often speaks on behalf of his king and is given authority over others. This illustrates the special role assigned to this elect nation of God. Through this blessed people comes the manifestations

---

[93] Marshall, 123.

[94] Alfred Jones teaches that the mysterious verb שרה might very well mean "to be princely," and assumes that the name Israel consists of a future form of this verb, which hence would mean to become princely. And so Jones interprets the name Israel with He Will Be Prince With God. Alfred Jones, *Jones' Dictionary of Old Testament Proper Names* (London: Kregel Publications, 1997), 130.

of God, His promises, His law, His covenants, and most significantly His only-begotten Son, the Word.

In other words, there is a blessing to being an Israelite, but not all of the Israelites are chosen to carry that blessing. Not all Israelites are given to be prophets or apostles to bring the Word to the world. Not every Jew will be in the lineage of the Messiah or be entrusted to carry His message. So, there is a benefit to being a Jew, but not every Jew has been chosen for that benefit.

As will become clear in this study, some of these Israelites were left in their calloused condition for the ignoble purpose of crying out "crucify Him" on the day the Lord's promise for redemption was fulfilled (Acts 2:23). Some Jews were given a "spirit of stupor" to blind them from the clearly-revealed truth of their own Messiah's identity (Rom. 11:8, Mark 4:11, Matt. 11:25, Luke 19:42). This interpretation is consistent with Jesus's comment,

> **Luke 19:41-42:** "As he approached Jerusalem and saw the city, he wept over it and said, 'If you, even you, had only known on this day what would bring you peace—but now it is hidden from your eyes.'"

Is it fair that God had chosen to entrust some unfaithful Israelites to bring His Word, while blinding other equally-unfaithful Israelites from seeing it in order to fulfill His redemptive promise?[95] Paul writes Romans 9–11 to explain to his audience why this is not only just, but abundantly merciful (Rom. 11:32).[96]

---

[95] Please see chapter 4 for further explanation on the Judicial hardening of Israel.

[96] I. Howard Marshall, Stephen Travis and Ian Paul, *Exploring the New Testament: A Guide to the Letters and Revelation, Vol. 2* (Downers Grove, IL: IVP Academic, 2011), 124-125.

Romans 9:6–8

It is not as though God's Word had failed. For not all who are descended from Israel are Israel. Nor because they are His descendants are they all Abraham's children. On the contrary, "It is through Isaac that your offspring will be reckoned." In other words, it is not the children by physical descent who are God's children, but it is the children of the promise who are regarded as Abraham's offspring.

This passage cannot be separated from Paul's opening remarks. Some readers misinterpret the "amen" that concludes verse 5 to mean "the end." For the early church, the term "amen" does not bring an end to a thought but declares a hope that the thought never ends. Paul continues in the same line of reasoning despite the paragraph break and new title heading added by many modern translations. In fact, the conjunction *de* ("but" or "moreover") which begins this sentence clearly confirms Paul's thought has not been broken from the previous verses.

The purpose for God electing and blessing Israel (vs. 5) has not failed (vs. 6). This is the same objection introduced by Paul in Rom. 3:3, "What if some were unfaithful? Will their unfaithfulness nullify God's faithfulness?" In other words, will the unbelief of most Israelites thwart the Potter's promise to Abraham that "all peoples on earth will be blessed through you?" (Gen. 12:3b).

It might appear to a first-century audience that God's plan for Israel to bring God's Word to the rest of the world was a huge failure. Most Jews, especially the notable leaders, stood in direct opposition to the word of God, yet it was known that God had chosen Israel to be entrusted with His Word (Rom. 3:2b). In fact, it was because God chose Israel as His mouthpiece that the Jews earned their nickname, "the elect of God." As Rom. 9:4–5 indicates, from them was the law, the prophets, the Scriptures, and the patriarchs, but has that now come to a complete halt? Is God no longer revealing His Word through Israel? Has God's Word failed? Has the Potter broken His promise to Abraham?

This point is key in understanding the rest of Paul's argument throughout the next three chapters. One cannot overemphasize how vital it is to rightly understand the question Paul is attempting to answer at this point in his letter. Many well-intending biblical scholars throughout history have failed to follow Paul's line of thought in this contested passage leading them to erroneous conclusions.[97]

Confusion over some of Paul's writings is not new. The apostle Peter warns that some of Paul's teachings were difficult to understand and could be misinterpreted (2 Pet. 3:16). If an inspired apostle, known to be associated with the church in Rome, came to this conclusion about Paul's teaching, it would be wise for all Christians to tread carefully.

The fact that the "Calvinistic" interpretations of Paul's writings do not appear until the fifth century with Augustine should be of considerable concern, especially given that Augustine did not speak Greek and

---

[97] James White states, "Only one issue needs to be raised regarding the previous sections: the key to the passage that I hardly ever see addressed by non-Reformed exegetes is the relationship between 9:6 and the rest of the chapter. Paul is addressing one particular issue in this passage, that being, how is it that so many of Abraham's physical descendants reject the Messiah? Why do the great body of Jews reject their Messiah? This is a personal question. Paul, as a Jew, embraced the Messiah personally. Most of his brethren rejected Christ personally. Why? This issue is paramount." James White, "A Reformed Response to the Comments of R. C. H. Lenski on Romans 9," Quote taken from: http://vintage. aomin.org/Lenskirep.html; [date accessed 4/22/15].

was known to be former Manichean Gnostic,[98] a group that promoted deterministic philosophy and was notorious for its fights with the early church fathers.[99]

While St. Augustine contributed many good writings (some of which support libertarian free will), his unique perspective on election and predestination has been a point of contention sense they were first introduced.[100] Given that the Augustinian interpretations have led to unique conflicts throughout the history of the Western church, it would be wise to take a closer objective look into their source of origin.[101]

---

[98] John Calvin admits that his theology was first clearly seen in Augustine. How did Augustine arrive at his views on election and predestination, which were not consistent with the church's teaching for the first 300 years? It should be noted that Augustine was himself a Gnostic Manichaean for nearly a decade before converting to Catholicism. Calvin wrote, "Augustine is so wholly with me, that if I wished to write a confession of my faith, I could do so with all fullness and satisfaction to myself out of his writings." John Calvin, "A Treatise on the Eternal Predestination of God," in *John Calvin, Calvin's Calvinism,* trans. Henry Cole (Reformed Free Publishing Association, 1987), 38.

[99] The Manichaeans represent the Persian branch of Gnosticism, and they taught both determinism and total depravity. However, their determinism was based upon dualistic mythology. Hans Jonas, *The Gnostic Religion* (Beacon Press, 1958), 227.

[100] Loraine Boettner writes: "It may occasion some surprise to discover that the doctrine of Predestination was not made a matter of special study until near the end of the fourth century. The earlier church fathers placed chief emphasis on good works such as faith, repentance, almsgiving, prayers, submission to baptism, etc., as the basis of salvation. They of course taught that salvation was through Christ; yet they assumed that man had full power to accept or reject the Gospel. Some of their writings contain passages in which the sovereignty of God is recognized; yet along side of those are others which teach the absolute freedom of the human will. Since they could not reconcile the two they would have denied the doctrine of Predestination and perhaps also that of God's absolute Foreknowledge. They taught a kind of synergism in which there was a co-operation between grace and free will. It was hard for man to give up the idea that he could work out his own salvation. But at last, as a result of a long, slow process, he came to the great truth that salvation is a sovereign gift which has been bestowed irrespective of merit; that it was fixed in eternity; and that God is the author in all of its stages. This cardinal truth of Christianity was first clearly seen by Augustine, the great Spirit-filled theologian of the West. In his doctrines of sin and grace, he went far beyond the earlier theologians, taught an unconditional election of grace, and restricted the purposes of redemption to the definite circle of the elect." Loraine Boettner, *"Calvinism in History,"* Quote taken from: http://ww-w.monergism.com/thethreshold/sdg/boettner/boettner_calvinism.html; [date accessed 4/12/15].

[101] James Leo Garrett wrote, "From Augustine of Hippo to the twentieth century, Western Christianity has tended to interpret the doctrine of election

Despite what some suggest, Paul does not appear to be answering the question, "Since most Jews remain in unbelief, has the word of God failed in effectually saving the Jews?" Instead, he is more likely asking, "Has God's Word failed since those chosen to carry it are standing in opposition to it?"

Objections Anticipated

Does Romans 9 have nothing to do with salvation?

Romans 9 does involve salvation. God's redemptive plan, promised to Abraham, is channeled through Israel. No one is saved apart from the fulfillment of God's promise. If God's Word fails to come through Israel, then no individual in the world has any hope of salvation.

God unconditionally chose a nation and many individuals from that nation to bring about His redemptive plan. Apart from that plan being fulfilled, God cannot justly choose to save anyone who repents and believes. God freely bestows His saving grace to whomsoever He chooses solely because of the redemptive work of Christ brought to pass by His purpose in election.

When some hear the word election they immediately think that individuals were chosen for effectual salvation before creation, but even Calvinistic scholars must admit that not all biblical references to election

---

from the perspective of and with regard to individual human beings. During those same centuries the doctrine has been far less emphasized and seldom ever controversial in Eastern Orthodoxy. Is it possible that Augustine and later Calvin, with the help of many others, contributed to a hyper individualization of this doctrine that was hardly warranted by Romans 9–11, Eph. 1, and I Peter 2? Is it not true that the major emphasis in both testaments falls upon an elect people—Israel (OT) and disciples or church (NT)?" James Leo Garrett Jr., *Systematic Theology: Biblical Historical, and Evangelical, Vol. 2* (Grand Rapids: Eerdmans, 1995), 500.

are rightly understood in this manner.[102] God elects nations and individuals to carry out both noble and ignoble purposes in His redemptive plan without regard to the morality of those involved. Likewise, He chooses where His message will be sent without regard to the morality of the people hearing it (Jonah 1:2; Matt. 22:10).

God often makes choices unconditioned upon the character or desires of those involved (Rom. 9:16). When approaching the Scripture one must seek to discern what kind of divine choice is being referenced, without merely assuming every choice of God is about individuals being elected unto effectual salvation.

Does Romans 9 not have individuals in view?

Individuals are very much in view throughout Romans 9. Acknowledging the national components clearly evident in this passage does not negate the reference to the individuals involved. Some Calvinists may assume that the non-Calvinistic corporate interpretation avoids any reference to the individuals within the corporate group. However, the corporate interpretation actually involves more individuals than the interpretation the typical Calvinist is seeking to defend.

When interpreting Romans 9, Calvinists are forced to change their hermeneutical approach from an individual application of salvation to a corporate application somewhere before they get to the end of the chapter and into the following two chapters. Otherwise, they have the dilemma of explaining why the

---

[102] John Piper states, "And since the church is not an ethnic group like Israel was, God doesn't elect a whole nation for earthly purposes like He did Israel at the Red Sea." John Piper, "The Pleasure of God in Election." Quote taken from: http://www.desiringgod.org/sermons/the-pleasure-of-godin-election; [date accessed 4/15/16].

same individually-hardened Israelites who are stumbling have not stumbled beyond recovery or the hope of being grafted back in for salvation (Rom. 11:11–23).

The context of Romans 9 involves individuals and covers the topics of election and salvation, but the context must be examined in order to understand the apostle's intention. Jews had come to believe that eternal life was guaranteed to any law-abiding citizen of Israel simply on the basis of their being of Israel. They wrongly assumed that being the elect people of God secured their own individual salvation. Ironically, the root of this same erroneous conclusion still leads many to misinterpret Paul's intentions. Israel was elected to carry the word of God so that anyone might believe and be blessed. Israelites were not guaranteed salvation on the basis of being a descendant of Abraham.

The question Paul is asking is this: *If God has entrusted His Word to the Israelites (vv. 4–5) and the Israelites are standing in opposition to His Word (vv. 2–3), then has God's promise to deliver His Word through Israel failed (vs. 6)?* Paul's answer is twofold. Not every descendant of Israel is entrusted with the words of God, nor is everyone who is a child of God made a child on the basis that he or she is a natural descendent of Abraham. Consider the apostle's response in Romans 9:6.

Romans 9:6
It is not as though God's Word had failed. For not all who are descended from Israel are Israel.

God's Word has not failed to come through Israel because not everyone from Israel has been given the noble purpose of bringing that Word (vv. 5, 21).[103] In other words, not every individual descendant of Abraham is chosen to accomplish what the nation of Israel was chosen to accomplish. Moreover, not every descendant of Israel is chosen to carry out the purpose for which God elected Israel.

Calvinists typically read this phrase to mean God has elected effectually to save some Israelites ("true Israel"), not all of them ("reprobates").[104] This approach, however, does not adequately address the real question of God's Word being entrusted to Israel (vv. 4-5) so as to bring the promise of redemption for the whole world (v. 6).

Consider this analogy: What if we allowed Jonah, the prophet, to represent the nation of Israel and Nineveh to represent the rest of the world. When Jonah was unfaithful to God, one may have asked: "Has God's Word failed?" The answer to that question is

---

[103] Some scholars refer to this "noble purpose" as God's "election to service." For example, Eric Hankins, the primary author of *A Traditional Southern Baptist Statement of God's Plan of Salvation*, presented his research at a conference stating, "Fred Klooster's treatment of the Biblical data concerning election in the *Evangelical Dictionary of Theology* is typical of most evangelical approaches to the subject. He notes that the Bible gives us a 'rich vocabulary to express several aspects' of election. He mentions specifically (1) elect angels, (2) election to service, (3) the election of Israel, (4) the election of Christ, and (5) election to salvation, with which, Klooster says 'the rest of this article is concerned.' Millard Erickson, in his systematic treatment of soteriology, acknowledges the frequency of corporate ideas of election and election to service in the Scripture, but waives these off to deal, as Klooster does, with only the idea of individual election to salvation. Grudem, in his systematic theology, does not even mention the Old Testament in laying out his Biblical basis for the doctrine of election. He assumes that determinism is the equivalent of election, so that's all he finds in the Scriptures. What warrant could there be in simply jettisoning the totality of the Biblical data? I frequently hear 'election to service' and 'corporate election' dismissed as sort of second class ideas concerning the doctrine, so we can all hurry to the discussion of how God chooses some individuals and not others. However, I think we are ignoring the lion's share of the Biblical data in doing so. What might election look like if we really allowed the Bible to speak?" Eric Hankins, audio presentation of the 2013 John 3:16 Conference, "Dr. Eric Hankins, 2013 John 3:16 Presentation, Part 2/3." Quote taken from: http://sbctoday.com/dr-eric-hankins-2013-john-316-presentation-part-23/; [date accessed: 1/3/16].

[104] John Piper, *The Justification of God* (Grand Rapids, MI: Baker Books, 1993), 85-92.

found by reviewing the story of Jonah. God sovereignly brings His Word through an unfaithful vessel. Likewise, God entrusts His Word to come through Israel who, like Jonah, was unfaithful. With this in mind, how might the apostle prove that God's Word has not failed despite the unfaithful vessel being entrusted to bring it? Paul simply retells the story of Israel and the Potter's faithfulness to fulfill His promise.

Romans 9:7-8a
Nor because they are his descendants are they all Abraham's children. On the contrary, it is through Isaac that your offspring will be reckoned. That is, it is not the children of the flesh who are children of God...

God never promised to save anyone on the basis of his or her nationality, so how could that promise have failed? One does not become a child of God simply on the basis of being a child of Abraham. People are saved by grace through faith, not their nationality or their works. God shows mercy to whomever He desires to show mercy, and He desires to show mercy to those who humbly admit they cannot earn righteousness by works, regardless of their nationality. He does not desire to save anyone based upon his or her relationship to Abraham (Rom. 2:17-29).

Calvinists make the mistake of assuming Paul is merely restating the same point in two different ways. The only point, according to Calvinism, is that God has not chosen to effectually save every Israelite, but only a select few from Israel.[105] Again, this approach only

---

[105] John Piper states, "Second, in verse 7a he says it a little differently, but makes the same point: 'Nor are they all children because they are Abraham's descendants.' In other words, he is distinguishing here between two kinds of 'children' – there are all of Abraham's descendants, and there is a narrower

serves to answer one of Paul's dilemmas and in doing so it creates many other unnecessary questions and contradictions.

If God's election of Jacob is completely unconditional then he would not have needed to be Isaac's son; he could have been any random child in the world. God specifically chose Jacob to fulfill the promise He made to his grandfather, just like the rest of Israel (Deut. 7:8). If one presumes this choice is about individual salvation, then one promotes the view that God chooses effectually to save people based on promises made to their parents rather than upon their own response to the revelation of God, which denies individual responsibility and promotes fatalistic rationalizations of being born a victim in the wrong family. So, while the choice of one brother over the other may not have been based on their morality (vs. 11),[106] it certainly was contingent upon his being a child in the lineage of Abraham, which makes the choice conditional and the Calvinistic perspective flawed at its very core.

The choice of Jacob over Esau was for the purpose of fulfilling God's promise to Abraham (the promise to bring a blessing to all, not a promise to save some of his children and damn the rest of them unconditionally). Whosoever blessed Abraham, or his lineage in fulfilling that promise, regardless of their family background, would likewise be blessed (Gen. 12:3). God's gracious blessing, like our salvation today, came by grace alone through faith alone.

---

group in that number whom he calls here 'the children,' or we could say, 'the true children' since the others are physical children also." John Piper, "God's Word Stands: Not All Israel Is Israel, Part 1," Quote taken from: http://www.desiringgod.org/sermons/gods-word-stands-not-all-israel-is-israel-part-1; [date accessed 4/2/15].

[106] F. F. Bruce, *Tyndale New Testament Commentaries: The Letter of Paul to the Romans, Revised Edition* (Grand Rapids, MI: Eerdmans Publishing, 1994), 178.

Romans 9:8b
...it is the children of the promise who are regarded as Abraham's offspring.

The word *logizomai* ("regarded") indicates what God is presently and continually doing (since it is third person singular present deponent middle). That is, He is reckoning, counting, or choosing children based on their faith connection to His promise. The word *teknon* ("children") is plural and could be nominative (subject) or accusative (object). Rarely is this noun, when plural nominative/accusative, used with a singular verb. But even if it is the subject of the sentence here and this verb's inflected form is taken in an unusual way as a passive, the question still points to who is "regarding" them as "children" and why. Clearly, God is counting individuals as His children based upon their faith in His promise, just as He has done throughout all of human history.[107]

This verb would have to be in the perfect tense to support the Calvinistic premise that God has "regarded" (or chosen) His elect before the foundation of the world to be children of the promise. It does not help their argument if Paul is saying that God is regarding them that way presently in response to their faith in that promise.

Because Calvinists interpret Paul's question wrongly they unintentionally misapply his answer in support of their faulty premise. If the question is, *"Has God's Word failed effectually to save every Israelite?"* then the answer appears to be, *"No, because God wanted to save effectually only some Israelites."* So the Calvinist interprets Paul's words, "For not all who

---

[107] Gen. 12:3; Rom. 4:3; 2 Pet. 2:7. Personal notes from Brian Wagner Ph.D., professor of Biblical Languages at Virginia Bible College.

are descended from Israel are Israel" (9:6b) to mean "For they are not all effectually chosen for salvation who are descended from Israel," which means that God does not really desire the salvation of all the natural descendants of Israel, a view many Calvinists are not even willing to openly affirm.

The Calvinistic interpretation would undercut Paul's expressions of self-sacrificial love and patient long-suffering for all the descendants, including those being hardened. Likewise, it would bring into question every biblical expression of God's longing desire for all to come to faith and repentance (Rom. 9:1–3, 10:1, 21; 2 Pet. 3:9; 1 Tim. 2:4; Ezek. 18:32; Hos. 3:1).

Five-point Calvinists believe Paul is attempting to answer his imaginary questioner by teaching that God has only chosen to save effectually some Israelites while hardening all others from birth to certain condemnation. Such an interpretation does not align with either the immediate context or the whole of Scripture. In fact, such an interpretation pits God's desires against the desires expressed by the apostle in Rom. 9:1–3 and in 10:1. In other words, consistent Calvinists must conclude that God's desires are in opposition to the desires expressed by Paul while writing under divine inspiration.

Moreover, Rom. 10:21 is not merely Paul's expressed desire for the unbelieving Jews, but a direct quote from the mouth of God Himself. Thus, the Calvinistic interpretation introduces a supposed secret divine desire that stands in direct opposition to the clearly-expressed desires of the inspired apostle and God Himself.

Paul is not attempting to teach that only some Israelites have been chosen for salvation before the foundation of the world, but that (1) the fulfillment of God's promise to Abraham is not dependent upon the faithfulness of his descendants; and (2) no Israelite has been chosen for salvation on the basis that he or she is an ethnic Israelite. How does the apostle go about making his case? He points the audience back to God's promise:

> **Gen. 12:2-3:** "And I will make you a great nation, And I will bless you, And make your name great; And so you shall be a blessing; And I will bless those who bless you, And the one who curses you I will curse. And in you all the families of the earth will be blessed."

Romans 9:9–12
> **For this is the word of promise: 'At this time I will come, and Sarah shall have a son.' And not only this, but there was Rebekah also, when she had conceived twins by one man, our father Isaac; for though the twins were not yet born and had not done anything good or bad, so that God's purpose according to His choice would stand, not because of works but because of Him who calls, it was said to her, 'The older will serve the younger.'**

God chose Isaac, not Ishmael, to be the one through whom the promise was fulfilled. What is that promise? Does God promise Abraham to save some of his individual children through effectual means but not others? Such a view is nowhere found in the text.[108]

If these passages mean that God has chosen individually Abraham's eldest son (Ishmael) and eldest

---

[108] "From the birth oracle to Rebekah (Gn. 25:23). The prophecy relates not to the individuals Esau and Jacob (for Esau never rendered service to Jacob) but to their descendants; it relates to the long periods during which the Edomites were in servitude to Israel or Judah (cf. 2 S. 8:14; 1 Ki. 22:47; 2 Ki. 14:7; etc.)." F. F. Bruce, 182.

grandson (Esau) to be damned to eternal torment before they were born, then how would that be fulfilling
God's stated promise, "I will bless you?" Any loving
parent or grandparent would rather be cursed himself
than live with such a "blessing."

In addition, the Calvinistic interpretation not only
undermines Paul's opening premise of self-sacrificial
love for one's enemies, it even goes so far as to undermine God's love for the unborn children of someone
He supposedly loves and vows to bless. This simply
does not fit with the nature of God as revealed in Christ
(Matt. 5:43–48) or in the other writings of Paul (Rom.
12:14).

The promise given to Abraham is to bring the
Word through his lineage so as to bless all those who
believe. When God says that "in you all the families of
the earth will be blessed," he is referring to His promise to bring the Word (the Messiah and His message)
to all peoples through the nation of Israel. Ishmael and
his descendants (Ishmaelites) were not chosen to fulfill that promise. Esau and his descendants (Edomites)
were not chosen to fulfill that promise. Jacob and his
descendants (Israelites) are chosen to fulfill that
promise, and God is just to make this choice despite
the fact that all three are direct descendants of Abraham.

Now to the positive side of God's elective purpose
seen in His choice of Jacob, the patriarchal head of Israel. God indicates that His choice is not due to anything impressive about the individual national head,
Jacob (Gen. 25:23), or the nation he represents (Deut.
7:7). God does not select individuals or nations to
carry out His promises based on how impressive they
appear. In fact, Scripture reveals just the opposite.

If His chosen army is too impressive, God will
downsize it to keep people from falsely believing they
gained the victory without His help (Judg. 6-8). God

often chooses the weak, unimpressive, and lowly through which to accomplish His purposes and plans.

Esau was the more likely choice of the two brothers given his natural qualities as a hunter and his being the firstborn. Jacob was the weaker, or lesser, of the two brothers and certainly not more deserving to carry out this noble purpose.

The point is that God did not choose to save one of them and condemn the other prior to their birth, as some attempt to read into this text. Instead, He chose to make His power known through the weaker, less likely candidate (just like He did with young David, 1 Sam. 16:7). We must understand that this gracious Potter most often chooses spoiled clay to fulfill His promises.

How does this point answer the original question posed by Paul in verse 6? It may appear to Paul's audience that God's promise to Israel had failed due to the low numbers of Israelites and the lack of notoriety of those Israelites who were affirming Christ as Israel's Messiah. Has not God previously fulfilled His promise through a small and insignificant remnant (Rom. 11:5)? Is God not faithful to accomplish what He promises, even if the odds seem to be against Him? Will the faithlessness of the majority of His chosen nation deter God from accomplishing His redemptive promise through them—even despite them? The apostle argues that God has never failed to accomplish His purpose throughout Israel's history, so why would He fail now (Rom. 3:3-4)? The Potter will fulfill His promise, regardless of the flaws in His chosen lump of clay (namely Israel). Paul explains,

> **Gal. 4:22-25:** "For it is written that Abraham had two sons, one by the slave woman and the other by the free woman. His son by the slave woman was born according to the flesh, but his

son by the free woman was born as the result of a divine promise. These things are being taken figuratively: The women represent two covenants. One covenant is from Mount Sinai and bears children who are to be slaves: This is Hagar. Now Hagar stands for Mount Sinai in Arabia and corresponds to the present city of Jerusalem, because she is in slavery with her children."

The typical Calvinistic interpretation appears to take Romans 9 literally to suggest that the son (Ishmael) of the slave woman (Hagar) is condemned under the law before being born and doing anything sinful.[109] This may have been a valid interpretation had the apostle Paul not clearly explained his teaching as being figurative or allegorical. Some Calvinist's interpretation of Romans 9 literalizes an allegory, thus failing to understand Paul's intended meaning.[110]

Paul's continued dialogue to include the choice of Jacob over Esau likewise carries this same national symbolic meaning as reflected in the quote from Gen. 25:23, "Two nations are in your womb; And two peoples will be separated from your body..." Clearly, the apostle is using God's choice of Isaac and Jacob over Ishmael and Esau as a representation of God's choice to save those under the covenant of faith rather than the covenant of law.

Romans 9:13
Just as it is written, Jacob I loved, but Esau I hated.

---

[109] James Montgomery Boice, *Romans, 4 vols.* (Grand Rapids: Baker, 1991), 3:1094.

[110] "The 'children of the promise' in Paul's exegesis are those who, like Abraham, believe the promise of God and are therefore Abraham's spiritual offspring. Compare 4:11-18 and also the 'allegory' which Paul draws out of the Isaac-Ishmael narrative in Galatians 4:22-31." F. F. Bruce, 182.

This text does not teach that God hated an unborn baby for no apparent reason, as some interpret it to mean.[111] Paul quotes from Genesis in Rom. 9:11–12 and then quotes from Malachi in Rom. 9:13. Between these texts, from the first and last books of the Old Testament, is a period of more than 1500 years. Paul was providing a before and after statement, not a new interpretation of the Old Testament.

Both of the twins were gone before the house of Esau (Edomites) invoked the curse of God's expressed hatred (Mal. 1:2-3). The expressed angst against Esau's descendants is also found in the book of Obadiah. Here one sees the true cause of God's expressed hatred toward these people:

Obad. 1:10: "Because of the violence against your brother Jacob, you will be covered with shame; you will be destroyed forever."

Mal. 1:2-3: "'I have loved you,' says the Lord. But you ask, 'How have you loved us?' 'Was not Esau Jacob's brother?' declares the Lord. 'Yet I have loved Jacob, but Esau I have hated, and I have turned his hill country into a wasteland and left his inheritance to the desert jackals.'"

Malachi recorded this curse hundreds of years after Jacob and Esau lived on earth. Both Malachi and Obadiah reflect on Edom's attacks against Israel throughout their writings, giving a clear cause for

---

[111] Calvinist John Hendryx writes, "The bible is clear that just as God chooses some for mercy and salvation, He chooses others for Judicial hardening and reprobation: when He loved Jacob, even before his birth, He also hated Esau at the same time (Rom. 9:10–13)." John Hendryx, "What is 'double predestination,' and does the bible teach it?" Quote taken from: http://www.monergism.com/thethreshold/articles/onsite/qna/double.html; [date accessed: 12/14/15].

God's declared hatred for Esau, which was directed against his posterity, the Edomites. It is also clear from the original references that individual salvation was not in view, but national blessing (because of the references to Edom's land and inheritance, rather than an individual's eternal destiny).

To support their premise, Calvinists must assume that Paul engages in eisegetical proof-texting in order to make a case for the unconditional election of individuals for effectual salvation, a concept foreign to the Old Testament. It is clear, however, that Paul was simply summarizing this historical account by speaking of God's prophecy for the twins and the nations they represent. Then, going on to reveal the final outcome of Edom's rebellion and God's subsequent declaration of hatred. Never once is God's hatred expressed toward the unborn.[112]

What was Paul attempting to prove? Consider again the question posed in verse 6. Has God's Word failed since so many descendants of Abraham are standing in opposition to it? Paul answers with a resounding "No!" Esau's descendants, though of Isaac's own seed, stood in opposition against Israel and thus were cursed in accordance with God's original promise to Abraham, "the one who curses you I will curse" (Gen. 12:3), which was a conditional response of God against people who freely chose to attack those carrying out His promise. It was not an unconditional choice to reprobate an unborn baby for His own Self-glorification — a gross misrepresentation of God's holy character and self-sacrificial love for all people.

Paul's quote from Malachi of God's hatred for the Edomites, which are referred to by their patriarchal head as "Esau" (a common practice in that culture, Gen. 36:43), was an obvious reflection of God's curse

---

[112] See the appendix for more on this topic.

against anyone who opposes the fulfillment of God's redemptive promise, even if they are direct descendants of Isaac himself.[113]

God told Israel, "You shall not detest an Edomite, for he is your brother" (Deut. 23:7). In light of this explicit divine instruction, are readers to believe God himself unconditionally detested Jacob's brother Esau, and the nation of Edom, from before the foundation of the world for no apparent reason?

Also, one learns from the text that Jacob loved his elder brother and reconciled with him, saying to him, " . . . if now I have found favor in your sight, then take my present from my hand, for I see your face as one sees the face of God" (Gen. 33:10). In Exodus 20, God instructs Israel to respect the Edomite boundaries because they are relatives and have been given their land as a divine blessing. It is only after the Edomites attack Israel that God curses them, as was conditionally promised in God's first encounter with Abraham, "I will curse those who curse you" (Gen. 12:3).

The most common Calvinistic interpretation of God hating Esau unto eternal damnation from birth simply does not fit the context of either the Old Testament narrative or of the apostle's letter to the first-century church in Rome.[114]

---

[113] "From Malachi 1:2-3, where again the context indicates it is the nations Israel and Edom, rather than their individual ancestors Jacob and Esau, that are in view. The way in which communities can be so freely spoken of in terms of their ancestors is an example of the common oscillation in the Biblical (and especially Old Testament) thought and speech between individual and corporate personality. Israel was the elect nation, and Edom incurred the wrath of God for its unbrotherly conduct towards Israel in the day of Israel's calamity." F. F. Bruce, 182.

[114] Some Calvinists argue against equal ultimacy (sometimes called "double predestination"). According to R. C. Sproul Sr., "Equal ultimacy is the view that: God works in the same way and same manner with respect to the elect and to the reprobate. That is to say, from all eternity God decreed some to election and by divine initiative works faith in their hearts and brings them actively to salvation. By the same token, from all eternity God decrees some to sin and damnation and actively intervenes to work sin in their lives, bringing them to

If Paul's intent in verses 11-13 was not to say that God has rejected many before they were born, then what was he trying to say? What other reason might Paul have to reference Esau and the Edomites?

Remember the false belief of the Israelites in Paul's day who assumed they were going to be saved simply on the basis that they were descendants of Abraham? Paul is proving that God's promise includes cursing those who opposed the fulfillment of that promise, even if they are of Isaac's seed. In short, being the seed of Isaac does not ensure your salvation, especially if you stand in opposition to the Word of God, as did the Edomites.

Paul attempts to demonstrate that descendants of Abraham have been fighting those who were carrying the promise since the very beginning. This point would bolster Paul's contention that God's promise to Israel has not failed, although many of Abraham's descendants are standing in active opposition, just as Edom had done before them. God's curse, or hatred, against

---

damnation by divine initiative. In the case of the elect, regeneration is the monergistic work of God. In the case of the reprobate, sin and degeneration are the monergistic work of God. This distortion of positive-positive predestination clearly makes God the author of sin who punishes a person for doing what God monergistically and irresistibly coerces man to do. Such a view is indeed a monstrous assault on the integrity of God. This is not the Reformed view of predestination, but a gross and inexcusable caricature of the doctrine. Such a view may be identified with what is often loosely described as hyper-Calvinism and involves a radical form of supralapsarianism. Such a view of predestination has been virtually universally and monolithically rejected by Reformed thinkers." R.C. Sproul, "Double Predestination." Quote taken from: http://www.thehighway.com-/Double Predestination_Sproul.html; [date accessed 4/26/15]..

But, a Calvinistic interpretation of Romans 9 would be hard pressed to remain consistent in explaining how the active work of God in loving Jacob is not ultimately equal to his hating of Esau (vs. 13) given that it was supposedly a monergistic action prior to the twin's birth. So too, the active work of "mercying" in contrast to hardening as interpreted by many Calvinists in verse 18 certainly appears to meet the "radical form of supralapsarianism" as defined by Sproul above. If mankind's natural condition of total inability is brought to pass by sovereign decree, which no Calvinist could consistently deny, then how can the charge of equal ultimacy be denied with anything more than a distinction without a difference?

Esau (Edom) for opposing God's Word carried by Jacob (Israel) served as a warning for all Abraham's current descendants, lest they meet the same condemning curse by opposing the Word of God now carried by chosen Israelites such as Paul.

In other words, Paul explains that being a descendant of Abraham will not ensure your salvation. In fact, any seed of Abraham who stands against the fulfillment of God's promise will stand cursed, or hated, by God. If you do not believe that truth, then just look at the Edomites, direct descendants of Isaac himself.

As discussed in chapter one, the term "hate" is sometimes an idiomatic expression of choosing one over another for a greater purpose, and certainly would not mean despise or reject without the possibility of reconciliation.[115] For instance, Jesus told Peter, "If anyone comes to me and does not hate his own father and mother and wife and children and brothers and sisters, yes, and even his own life, he cannot be my disciple" (Luke 14:26).

No reputable commentator would suggest the term hate in Luke 14:26 should be interpreted literally. If so, one would be hard pressed to explain Scripture's other teachings about loving and honoring one's parents. Instead, this passage should be understood to mean that individuals must choose to follow God's will over the will of even the most beloved in one's life. In other words, this is the idiomatic way of communi-

---

[115] Greek scholars explain how the Greek word "hate" (miseo) does not necessarily mean "an active abhorrence," but means "to love less." E. W. Bullinger described the word "hate" as hyperbole and rendered the word as meaning "does not esteem them less than me" E. W. Bullinger, *Figures of Speech Used in the Bible* (Grand Rapids, MI: Baker, 1968), 426.

cating that one is to choose Christ and His noble purposes over one's parents and their common purposes.[116]

The same hermeneutical principle could be applied toward understanding God's choice of Jacob over Esau. God clearly chose one over the other for a noble purpose. Also, this interpretation does not pit Paul's expressed love for the hardened Jews against God's hatred, thus making the apostle appear more benevolent and self-sacrificial than the One who inspired his writings.

Further, one who follows the implications of a consistent Calvinistic interpretation would have to conclude that Ishmael was likewise hated and rejected by God before the creation of the world. However, Gen. 17:15–26 states,

> "Then God said to Abraham, 'As for Sarai your wife, you shall not call her name Sarai, but Sarah shall be her name. I will bless her, and indeed I will give you a son by her. Then I will bless her, and she shall be a mother of nations; kings of peoples will come from her.' Then Abraham fell on his face and laughed, and said in his heart, 'Will a child be born to a man one hundred years old? And will Sarah, who is ninety years old, bear a child?' And Abraham said to God, 'Oh that Ishmael might live before You!' ... 'As for Ishmael, I have heard you; behold, I will bless him, and will make him fruitful and will multiply him exceedingly. He shall become the father of twelve princes, and I will make him a great nation. But

---

[116] A. B. Bruce stated that "the practical meaning" of the word "hate" is "love less." A. B. Bruce, *Training of the Twelve "Principles for Christian Leadership,"* Brighton Christian Classic Series Book 6 (Grand Rapids, MI: Eerdmans, 1903), 575.

> My covenant I will establish with Isaac, whom Sarah will bear to you at this season next year.' When He finished talking with him, God went up from Abraham.... In the very same day Abraham was circumcised, and Ishmael his son."

Clearly, there is a distinction between Ishmael and Isaac, but one would be hard pressed to prove that Ishmael was hated and rejected based on the conditional blessing of God's original promise: "I will bless those who bless you" (Gen. 12:3). The biblical account draws a stark distinction between those chosen to bring the Word and those chosen through faith to be blessed by that Word.

Are we to believe that Isaac's six younger brothers likewise were born reprobates, since they too were passed over from carrying out the promise made to Abraham? There is no reason to suggest Abraham's other sons were not able to benefit from the conditional provision of the original promise through faith simply because they were not chosen to bring the Word to the world. The typical Calvinistic interpretation confounds the two distinct promises of God as if they are one, causing confusion about the biblical doctrine of election. The Potter's blessing given to his vessel Abraham and a particular lineage should be understood as distinct from His blessing of those who choose to believe in the Potter's promise.

Consider Abraham's beloved nephew Lot. He was not chosen to carry out the promise either. Like the Edomites, God also curses Lot's future descendants, the Moabites and Ammonites, for their opposition to Israel (Deut. 23:3). Must one conclude, despite Peter's declaration of Lot's righteousness (2 Pet. 2:7), that Lot was among the reprobate? If Lot meets the same descriptions seen in Esau, then why not? Is it only because Lot's descendants are not called the "Lotites" and referred to in the text by the name of their patri-archal head, or just that Paul did not use him and his posterity as the example to make his case against na-tional privilege?

If one considers others in the lineage, then Jacob's three eldest sons must likewise be taken into account. Reuben, Simeon, and Levi failed to receive the birth-right, but in this instance the reasons are given. Scrip-ture clearly indicates that Jacob refused to give the birthright to his three eldest sons due to their sinful actions (Gen. 49:1–7). Instead, the blessing was given to Judah (vs. 8). A strong distinction was made be-tween those blessed to bring the Word and those who may or may not choose to believe in that Word.

It is not consistent to interpret these passages as God's choice to effectually save one brother to the damning neglect of the others. While that interpreta-tion would serve to answer part of the original ques-tion posed in this chapter, it introduces unnecessary problems never intended by the author.[117]

Romans 9:14
What shall we say then? There is no injus-tice with God, is there? May it never be!

As noted before, many Israelites believed their in-dividual salvation was ensured on the basis of their na-tionality. They had come to believe that salvation was owed them simply because they were of Israel. Paul used their own Scripture to prove that a descendent of Abraham, or even Isaac: (1) might not be chosen for

---

[117] "Whether it be presented by Calvinists or Arminians, my contention is that this [Calvinistic] soteriological interpretation of the election in Romans 9 does not really address the question of God's righteousness, but rather com-pounds it. It does not address the question, because it does not even deal with the role of ethnic Israel as a whole, which is really what the problem is all about." Jack Cottrell, "Pharaoh as a Paradigm for Israel in Romans 9:18," (Evangelical Theological Society, 2003), 4.

the noble purpose of bringing the Word of God, and (2) might be cursed if he stands in opposition to those who had been chosen to carry His Word. As Robert Picirilli notes, "Those Jews would contend that God had unconditionally promised to save all Israel and would therefore be unrighteous if He failed to keep that promise." [118]

God is just to reject or curse (hate) any descendant of Isaac, the child of the promise. One needs only to examine the Scriptures to see what happened to Esau's descendants. God was just to condemn those decedents who opposed the fulfillment of God's promise; why would it be any different now? Picirilli rightly concludes,

> "The key to the passage is 9:14: 'Is there unrighteousness with God (in His treatment of Israel, which includes the present rejection of Israel)?' Paul's purpose for the three chapters is to answer this question with a resounding 'No.'"[119]

Paul has proven how God was just to condemn any descendent of Abraham for standing in opposition to the fulfillment of God's promise. Now, he shows how God is just to have mercy on other descendants who have been appointed to carry out His redemptive plan.[120]

Romans 9:15

---

[118] Robert Picirilli, *Grace, Faith, Free Will: Contrasting Views of Salvation: Calvinism and Arminianism* (Nashville: Randall House, 2002), 72.

[119] Ibid., 71.

[120] There was a common belief that God unconditionally promised every child of Abraham salvation. F. Forlines referred to this as the "Jewish problem." F. Leroy Forlines, *The Quest for Truth: Answering Life's Inescapable Questions* (Nashville: Randall House, 2001), 347.

For he says to Moses, I will have mercy on whom I have mercy, and I will have compassion on whom I have compassion.

Once again, Paul makes his case using a passage that would have been well known to Israelites of that day. Paul quotes from a conversation between God and Moses in Exodus 33. Israel had built a golden calf and God had determined to destroy them for their rebellion and begin again with Moses. Reminiscent of Paul's self-sacrificial appeal in the first three verses of Romans 9, Moses pleads with God, saying,

> **Exodus 32:31-32:** "Oh, what a great sin these people have committed! They have made themselves gods of gold. But now, please forgive their sin—but if not, then blot me out of the book you have written."

Though God relents, He remains angry at Israel and instructs Moses to travel into the Promised Land without Him lest He destroy the Israelites due to their stubbornness (Ex. 33:1-3). In Exodus 33:15–19, Moses again pleads with God.

At this point we must be reminded of the original question raised in Romans 9:4–6. *If the Israelites, the ones who had been entrusted with the very words of God, were unfaithful, then had God's Word failed?* Or, similarly stated earlier in chapter 3, "[Israelites] were entrusted with the oracles of God. What then? If some did not believe, their unbelief will not nullify the faithfulness of God, will it?" (Rom. 3:2-3).

Is there a better biblical example of God's faithfulness to carry out His promise through unfaithful Israelites than the story of Exodus 32 and 33? God's Words to Moses were a reaffirmation to fulfill His promise through Israel, although they deserved to be destroyed immediately.

Moses, a chosen type for the coming Messiah, interceded for unfaithful, calloused Israelites so that God's redemptive promise would be fulfilled through them (Deut. 18:18). Do Moses's self-sacrificial pleas for unfaithful Jews sound familiar? If not, then re-read Rom. 9:1–3.

Calvinists interpret verse 15 to mean that God can choose to save whomever He wishes, which is not a point any Traditionalist would deny. Whom God desires to save is no secret, however. Scripture declares plainly, "God resists the proud, but gives grace to the humble" (Jas. 4:6, 1 Pet. 5:5–6). God saves anyone He wishes to save and He wishes to save weak, humble, and repentant believers, regardless of their nationality (Ps. 18:27).

Paul was drawing upon the history of Israel to prove God's faithfulness to carry out His promise through them despite their unfaithfulness. In other words, Paul demonstrates how God continued to show mercy to Israel even when they were unfaithful and God did so in order to fulfill His original promise.

In short, God can choose to show mercy even to idol worshippers if He wishes. When it comes to fulfilling His promises to bring the provision of salvation to the world, He does what is necessary through chosen Israelites, whether by hardening some or "mercying" others. Therefore, fulfillment of the Potter's promise to Israel does not rest on the effort or desires of unfaithful Israelite vessels (Rom. 3:1-8).

Romans 9:16
So then it does not depend on the man who wills or the man who runs, but on God who has mercy.

What does "it" refer to in this verse? Calvinists assume that "it" refers to the individual, effectual salvation of unconditionally chosen people,[121] a concept nowhere introduced in this text or any other. Actually, "it" refers back to "God's purpose of election," (vs. 11) which is to fulfill the promise of God (vs. 6) in bringing about the redemptive plan through an unconditionally chosen nation of woefully unfaithful individuals.

Once again, this answers the original question posed by Paul in beginning of the chapter. *If God has entrusted His Word to the Israelites (vv. 4–5) and the Israelites are standing in opposition to His Word (vv. 2–3), then has God's Word failed (vs. 6)?* The apostle answers by reminding his readers that God's promise has never depended on the desires and efforts of unfaithful Israelites. The Potter's promise will be fulfilled despite and even through unfaithful vessels (Rom. 3:1-8).

Even further, Paul argues that God might use Israel's unfaithfulness to help bring about His redemptive promise. Paul's audience thinks Israel's unfaithfulness might thwart the fulfillment of God's Word (vs. 6), and Paul will reveal how God uses their unfaithfulness to accomplish His plan. To illustrate this point, Paul points back to the Scriptures.

God's redemptive plan through the narrative of Israel's exodus from slavery in Egypt is a foreshadowing of God's ultimate redemptive plan for the world (1 Cor. 10:10-12). Moses foreshadowed the coming Messiah, the one sent to rescue His people from slavery. But consider who Pharaoh was foreshadowing in the

---

[121] Calvinistic scholar William Shedd argues that "the ultimate reason why the individual believes, is that God elects him to faith, and produces it within him." William G. T. Shedd, *A Critical and Doctrinal Commentary on the Epistle of St. Paul to the Romans* (Grand Rapids: Zondervan, 1967), 271-272.

Exodus narrative. Although already a rebellious and Godless man, Pharaoh was blinded by God on several occasions throughout the story. Pharaoh was hardened in order to reveal the power of God and ensure the first Passover.[122]

Who was being hardened in the first century to demonstrate God's glory and ensure the real Passover? Ironically, it was the nation of Israel who was being hardened in the first century to accomplish God's redemptive plan (John 12:39–41; Acts 28:27). Although already a rebellious nation, Israel was blinded by God to ensure His promise was fulfilled.

Romans 9:17

For Scripture says to Pharaoh: 'I raised you up for this very purpose, that I might display my power in you and that my name might be proclaimed in all the earth.'

Paul uses the example of Pharaoh, a parallel to first-century Israel, to reveal how God has used the Jews' unfaithfulness to accomplish His promise. In the same manner that God blinded Pharaoh at times to ensure the first Passover, God likewise hardened Israel to ensure the real Passover. Notice the stated purpose in raising Pharaoh up (and later Israel) is not for condemnation, but in order to fulfill the word of God (vs. 6). This is not about the salvation or reprobation

---

[122] Jack Cottrell wrote, "Pharaoh is thus intended to serve as a paradigm for the nation of Israel. God has mercy on whom He wants to have mercy, i.e., He calls into His service whom He wants to call into His service; but some of these can serve His purposes only by being hardened. Thus it was with Pharaoh. God bestowed favor upon him by selecting him for a key role, but he could fill that role only by being hardened. And so it was with Israel also. God bestowed a temporal mercy upon them when He chose to use them in His redemptive plan, but He also hardened at least some of them (Rom. 11:7, 25) in reference to the role He wanted them to play." Jack Cottrell, *Pharaoh as a Paradigm for Israel in Romans 9:18*, (Cincinnati Bible Seminary Atlanta, GA: Evangelical Theological Society, 2003), 1-2.

of Pharaoh (or Israel); it is about the Potter's promise being fulfilled and His Word being made known to the whole earth even through unfaithful vessels.

The apostle is applying the Word of God about Pharaoh to the hardened Israelites of his own day. Paul was saying to the hardened Jews, not only has God's Word not failed due to your unfaithfulness, but God's Word is being fulfilled through your unfaithfulness, for He will demonstrate His power in you throughout all the earth.

God shows mercy to the Israelites in the Old Testament in order to accomplish His promise through them, and He hardens the Israelites in the New Testament in order to accomplish His promise through them. This explains Paul's statement in Romans 9:18.

Romans 9:18
Therefore God has mercy on whom He wants to have mercy, and He hardens whom He wants to harden.

Those judicially hardened and cut off are not born in this condition.[123] Rather, they are hardened after years of rebellion (Acts 28:27) and are cut off for their unbelief (Rom. 11:20). The hope of the apostle is that they might be grafted back in and saved (Rom. 11:11–32).

Remember the question Paul is answering: *Has God's promise to deliver His Word through unfaithful Israel failed?* No. In order to fulfill His promise and deliver His Word, God will show mercy to the unfaithful when necessary and He will harden the unfaithful

---

[123] Remember that non-Calvinistic scholars gladly affirm that God is free to show mercy to whomever He wishes. Picirilli says of Romans 9, "The purpose of verses 14-24 is to argue that the sovereign God is the one who determines who will be saved. . . . God still saves whom He wills and damns whom He wills, Jews or otherwise." Picirilli, Grace, 72.

when necessary. The fulfillment of God's promise does not depend on their faithfulness (Rom. 3:3). Whatever the Potter must do to fulfill His promise, He will do — even if that means blinding Israelites in their stubborn rebellion or compelling other sinful Israelites to carry His redemptive message to the world (Acts 9:1–19; Jonah).

In short, Israel's unfaithfulness does not thwart God's Word. Paul, like Jonah before him, was chosen to take God's Word to those on the outside. Both messengers needed convincing, but God did what was necessary to ensure His Word was delivered. He used external, persuasive means such as a big fish and a blinding light to accomplish this redemptive purpose, not inward, irresistible means. God's promise to deliver His Word through Israel did not depend on the messengers being faithful, which is exactly why God's Word has not failed (Rom. 9:6). His purpose in electing Israel will stand (Rom. 9:11).

Romans 9:19
One of you will say to me: 'Then why does God still blame us? For who is able to resist His will?'

Paul is saying: You (a Jew whom God has chosen to harden in his rebellion) will say to me (a Jew whom God has mercifully persuaded through external means to come out of his rebellion in order to fulfill God's promise): why does God blame me? For who resists His will? Paul is restating the same question posed in chapter 3: "But if our unrighteousness brings out God's righteousness more clearly, what shall we say? That God is unjust in bringing His wrath on us?" (Rom. 3:5). In other words, if the unrighteousness of the hardened Jew is a part of the Potter's plans to fulfill His promise, then why are the hardened vessels still to be blamed for their unrighteousness?

Paul's objector in chapters 3 and 9 is a Jew who has grown calloused in his rebellion (Acts 28:27) and is now being judicially hardened by God in order to accomplish His promise, which cannot fail (Rom. 9:6). It should be remembered that God never judicially hardens anyone who has not already grown hardened by his or her own free choice.[124] Nevertheless, the Judicial hardening spoken of here is an active and purposeful work of the Potter to prevent already calloused Israelites from recognizing their own Messiah for a time so as to fulfill His redemptive promise.[125]

The objector does not represent a totally depraved sinner born unable to respond to God and rejected as a reprobate before the foundation of the earth, as many Calvinists assume. Clearly, the lump of clay Paul

---

[124] John Stott, a Calvinistic scholar, quotes another Calvinist scholar in *Romans: God's Good News for the World* (Downers Grove: InterVarsity Press, 1994), 269, "Dr. Leon Morris rightly comments, 'Neither here nor anywhere else is God said to harden anyone who had not first hardened himself. That Pharaoh hardened his heart against God and refused to humble himself is made plain in the story. So God's hardening of him was a Judicial act, abandoning him to his own stubbornness, much as God's wrath against the ungodly is expressed by 'giving them over' to their own depravity (1: 24, 26, 28).'" John Piper, however, disagrees with Stott and Morris, stating in response to the quote above, "Let me say this calmly and firmly: That is exactly the opposite of what Romans 9:18 teaches." John Piper, "The Hardening of Pharaoh and the Hope of the World," Quote taken from: http://www.desiring-god.org/sermons/the-hardening-of-pharaoh-and-the-hope-of-the-world; [date accessed: 8/12/15].

[125] "Whatever answer we give to this question; we know that Paul was convinced that God partially hardened Israel so that blessing might come to the nations of the world...Whereas a traditional reading of Romans 9–11 has seen the hardening of non-remnant Israel as exclusively punitive in nature, the texts we have been exploring point in another direction...Also building upon Hays, Harink makes the theological implication thoroughly explicit: 'It is not possible to see Israel's present hardening as its unique (but unknowing) participation in the crucifixion of Jesus Christ.' While in Pauline language, Israel has experienced a 'partial hardening' that temporarily prevents her from corporately embracing Yeshua-faith, she nevertheless remains a holy people, set apart for God and God's purposes." Mark S. Kinzer, *Post-Messianic Judaism: Redefining Christian Engagement with the Jewish People* (Grand Rapids: Baker Books, 2005), 129–30, 135, 152.

will reference is not all of humanity born completely hardened in a condition Calvinists refer to as "Total Inability." Rather, the lump of clay is Israel, the topic of Paul's discourse from the very first sentence in this chapter. Thus, when the Traditionalist objects to the Calvinistic concept of total inability due to Adam's sin, it is a misrepresentation of the apostle's intentions to appeal to the following verses in defense of such a doctrine.

Romans 9:20–21
But who are you, a human being, to talk back to God? Shall what is formed say to the one who formed it, 'Why did you make me like this?' Does not the Potter have the right to make out of the same lump of clay some Pottery for special purposes and some for common use?

On the one hand, Calvinists will often reference this passage in order to argue that mankind has as much control over how he believes and behaves as a piece of clay has over its own shape, while on the other hand vehemently objecting to their opponent's accusations of making men into mere puppets. Some Calvinists want to have their cake and eat it too on this point. If they are going to interpret these biblical analogies in such a way that removes mankind's responsibility in the process, then they cannot object to another analogy which draws the exact same conclusion. After all, what more or less responsibility does a puppet have in relation to the puppet master than a lump of clay has in relation to the Potter on Calvinism's interpretation? If one wishes to interpret Paul's analogy of the Potter and the clay literally to mean that man has no say in how he believes and responds, then own it. Do not object to other analogies that draw the exact same implications unless you are not willing to live with those implications.

If the Calvinistic reading is flawed, then what is the more likely interpretation? First of all, who is bringing this objection? Some Calvinists would have us believe it was a first century "Arminian" (or "synergist") objecting to the idea that God chooses to condemn some people to hell before they ever do anything good or bad. But that interpretation simply ignores the context of the Scripture.

This is not the first time Paul anticipates this interlocutor's questions. Back in Romans 3:1-7, Paul goes through virtually the exact same diatribe as he does here in Romans 9. We specifically see the objector question God's wrath against those who are used to bring out God's righteousness,

> **Romans 3:5-6:** "But if our unrighteousness brings out God's righteousness more clearly, what shall we say? That God is unjust in bringing His wrath on us? (I am using a human argument.) Certainly not! If that were so, how could God judge the world?"

Generally speaking, Israel was a hell-bound lump of clay that had already grown calloused in self-righteous, legalistic religiosity (Acts 28:21-28). Despite their rebellion, the gracious Potter had patiently held out His hands to them for generations (Rom. 10:21). At times throughout Israel's history God shows mercy to calloused Israelites in order to fulfill His promise (Ex. 32-33), and at times He hardens them for the same purpose (Rom. 9-11).

At this time in history, despite the rebellion of Israel, the Divine Potter selects a portion from this spoiled lump of clay to carry His redemptive message to the rest of the world. This is to ensure His purpose for electing Israel will stand (Rom. 9:11).

The Potter remakes some of this lump for the noble purpose of carrying His Word to the rest of the world.[126] He uses persuasive signs, like a blinding light, to mold the wills of these otherwise rebellious messengers from Israel. He leaves the rest of this already-calloused lump in their rebellion, through which he accomplishes ignoble but necessary and redemptive purposes. Even still, the Potter holds out hope of their being provoked and grafted back in (Rom. 11:11-23).

In this text, Paul was likely drawing upon the analogy introduced by God through the prophet Jeremiah, which reads,

> **Jer. 18:1-6:** "This is the word that came to Jeremiah from the Lord: 'Go down to the Potter's house, and there I will give you my message.' So I went down to the Potter's house, and I saw Him working at the wheel. But the pot he was shaping from the clay was marred in His hands; so the Potter formed it into another pot, shaping it as seemed best to Him. Then the word of the Lord came to me. He said, 'Can I not do with you, Israel, as this Potter does?' declares the Lord. 'Like clay in the hand of the Potter, so are you in my hand, Israel.'"

Paul's fellow countrymen, like their fathers before them, were flawed pots in the hands of the Potter. It pleases the Potter to remake them into vessels to use for the accomplishment of His redemptive plan. Did the clay come to the Potter flawed already, or did the

---

[126] Gerhard Fredrich, ed., *Theological Dictionary of the New Testament, Vol. 7* (Grand Rapid, MI: Eerdmans Publishing, 1971), 362-363.

Potter Himself spoil the clay? If the clay represents all of humanity from birth, in accordance with His eternal decree, then it would imply that the Potter did the spoiling and the remaking. But if the clay is understood to represent Israel, then it is clear that the spoiling (or callousing) is a direct result of their own rebellious choices, not the molding of the Potter.

The Potter merely reshapes the already-flawed clay into something useful for a greater good, such as bringing the means of redemption to all peoples. Some vessels are selected to be used for noble purposes, like apostleship, while others are sealed in their calloused condition to fulfill God's redemptive plan. This indeed would give cause for all to glory in the free choices of such a righteous Potter sovereignly working to fulfill His promise.

The context of the Potter and clay analogy, recorded first in Jeremiah, sheds more light on the responsibility of the clay in relation to the Potter:

> **Jer. 18:7-12:** "If at any time I announce that a nation or kingdom is to be uprooted, torn down and destroyed, and if that nation I warned repents of its evil, then I will relent and not inflict on it the disaster I had planned. And if at another time I announce that a nation or kingdom is to be built up and planted, and if it does evil in my sight and does not obey me, then I will reconsider the good I had intended to do for it. Now therefore say to the people of Judah and those living in Jerusalem, 'This is what the Lord says: Look! I am preparing a disaster for you and devising a plan against you. So turn from your evil ways, each one of you, and reform your ways and your actions.' But they will reply, 'It's no use. We will continue with our own plans; we will all follow the stubbornness of our evil hearts.'"

Some Calvinistic scholars attempt to disassociate this text with Paul's use of the analogy in Romans. For instance, James White writes, "Where is there a discussion of vessels of honor and dishonor in Jeremiah 18? Where is there a discussion of vessels of wrath and vessels of mercy? There is none."[127]

Only someone set on dismissing human responsibility would be unwilling to acknowledge the clear connection. The vessels of honor can be seen in God's fashioning to "bless" (vs. 10), "build," and "plant" (vs. 9); while the vessels of dishonor can be seen in the fashioning to "uproot," "pull down" and "destroy" (vs. 7), including "fashioning calamity" and "devising a plan against" (vs. 11), which is also consistent with the Jewish hardening described in Romans chapter 9 and Romans 11:25.[128]

Paul is not oblivious to the need of the clay to respond to the expressed will of the Potter, as the apostle draws upon this analogy again in his letter to Timothy,

> **2 Tim. 2:20-21:** "Now in a large house there are not only gold and silver vessels, but also vessels of wood and of earthenware, and some to honor and some to dishonor. Therefore, *if anyone cleanses himself* from these things, he will be a vessel for honor, sanctified, useful to the Master, prepared for every good work" (emphasis added).

Clearly, the biblical authors speak of the clay as if it is able to respond (and thus be held responsible) to the will of the Potter.[129]

---

[127] James White, *The Potter's Freedom* (Amityville, NY: Calvary Press, 2000), 225.
[128] Notes from Richard Coords of www.examiningcalvinism.com
[129] Michael A. Harbin, *The Promise and the Blessing: A Historical Survey of the the Old and New Testaments* (Grand Rapids, MI: Zondervan, 2005), 518-519.

God, a patient and trustworthy Potter who genuinely loves the hardened clay (Rom. 9:1-2; 10:1, 21), has remade some of it to be used for noble purposes, such as proclaiming the inspired truth to the lost world. The rest of the lump, still genuinely loved by the Potter (Hos. 3:1), is used to bring about the ignoble purpose of crucifixion and the grafting in of other vessels for redemption (Rom. 11:25). All the while, the Potter is holding out hope for the spoiled lump to turn from its evil and be cleansed through repentance and faith (Rom. 11:11-23).

Romans 9:22

What if God, although choosing to show His wrath and make His power known, bore with great patience the objects of His wrath—prepared for destruction?

Although God clearly was willing to demonstrate His wrath on Israel after they built the golden calf, He mercifully endured in response to the pleading of Moses (Ex. 32-33). Israel was clearly fit for being destroyed after such rebellion, but God chose to show them mercy instead. As Paul concluded from the context of that narrative, "I will have mercy on whom I will have mercy."

Why does God refrain from displaying His wrath on Israel and show them mercy instead? Because Moses interceded on their behalf, much like Christ does for people today. God had a greater redemptive plan to accomplish through Israel, so He endured them even in their rebellion.

Just as God demonstrated His wrath and made His power known through Pharaoh's hardened unbelief, He likewise endured the calloused Israelites headed for destruction in order to demonstrate His mercy (Rom. 11:32). Just as Pharaoh and his army ended up destroyed at the bottom of the Red Sea, so too will be the fate of these hardened Jews if they do not leave their unbelief (Rom. 11:23). Like the Edomites, their brothers in the flesh before them, they will end up hated under the curse of the original promise if they remain in opposition to the Word of God (Rom. 9:13; Gen. 12:3).

Paul is not attempting to distinguish between those vessels blessed with effectual salvation and those vessels cursed with reprobation, as the Calvinists contend.[130] Instead, he is drawing a distinction between those vessels blessed to carry out the noble purpose of fulfilling God's promise and those vessels hardened in their rebellion in order to ensure the fulfillment of that same promise. In other words, it is all about the Potter's promise.

Paul is assured that these vessels, though stumbling, have not stumbled beyond hope of recovery (Rom. 11:11-14). The apostle Peter picks up on this same theme when he writes 2 Pet. 3:9–10, 14–16. Peter warned his readers not to be deceived by misapplied distortions of Paul's letters. He did so in the context of teaching "that patience is to be regarded as salvation," which could serve as an inspired commentary on Romans 9 itself.

Peter was known to have been an overseer in Rome followed sometime later by Clement of Rome, who has been identified as the one mentioned in Phil. 4:3. Tertullian tells us that Peter himself commissioned Clement.[131] Given that this letter was sent to the

---

130 According to John Piper, "Paul's concern is for the eternal destinies of those within the nation of Israel who are saved and who are accursed." John Piper, *The Justification of God*. 15, 71.

131 William Smith and Henry Wace, *A Dictionary of Christian Biography, Literature, Sects and Doctrines, Volume 1* (Boston: Little Brown and Company, 1877), 554.

church in Rome, it is reasonable to suggest that both Peter and Clement would have been familiar with its content. Some writings of Clement suggest his understanding of Paul's teaching was likewise in line with the present non-Calvinistic interpretation of divine election. For instance, he wrote,

> "It is therefore in the power of every one, since man has been made possessed of free-will, whether he shall hear us to life, or the demons to destruction. . . . He who is good by his own choice is really good; but he who is made good by another under necessity is not really good, because he is not what he is by his own choice. . . . For no other reason does God punish the sinner either in the present or future world, except because He knows that the sinner was able to conquer but neglected to gain the victory."[132]

Calvinistic historian, Loraine Boettner, concedes that the concept of individual effectual election to salvation "was first clearly seen by Augustine" in the fifth century. Not only did the earliest church fathers not interpret the doctrine of election "Calvinistically," much of their teaching stands in strong opposition to such a conclusion. A great emphasis on the absolute freedom of the human will and repudiations of individual predestination to salvation is found clearly throughout the earliest writings of the church.[133]

Romans 9:23–24

What if he did this to make the riches of His glory known to the objects of His

---

[132] Recognitions of Clement of Rome: III. 23, V. 8, IX. 30. Quote taken from: http://www.newadvent.org/fathers.htm; [date accessed: 10/12/15].

[133] Loraine Boettner, "Calvinism in History: Before the Reformation," Quote taken from: http://www.seeking4truth.com/before_reformation.html; [date accessed: 4/17/15].

mercy, whom He prepared in advance for glory—even us, whom He also called, not only from the Jews but also from the Gentiles?

Why has the Potter done all this? He is fulfilling His Word by bringing redemption to all the families of the earth. The Potter has made known the riches of His divine glory, which is best displayed through His benevolent mercy and self-sacrificial love expressed to all mankind upon the cross. The theme of self-sacrificial love is a thread that runs through the entirety of this passage and the whole of the gospel itself.

The first to trust in Christ from Israel, vessels remade for noble purposes and prepared for the glory to come, were not the only ones benefitting from the accomplishment of the Potter's redemptive plan. Gentiles, first introduced here in verse 24, were also to gain from the calloused rebellious actions of the hardened Jews. Through the sin of the hardened Israelite clay, salvation has come to the Gentiles (Rom. 11:11). And it is delivered to them by way of the gospel, carried by those remade from that same unfaithful lump of Jewish clay (Rom. 11:4).

Does conceding that God hardens Israel in their rebellion so as to accomplish redemption through them prove Calvinism is true? No, it proves that God judicially hardened already-calloused people in order to accomplish redemption for all people, including those who were being judicially hardened and could leave their unbelief once the hardening was lifted (Rom. 11:23, 32). It most certainly does not prove that all of humanity is born totally hardened by God and thus unable to see, hear, understand, and repent when confronted by the divinely-inspired gospel (2 Cor. 5:20).

Does conceding that God used persuasive means, like blinding lights and big fish in order to convince His messengers, prove that Calvinism is correct? No, it proves God uses persuasive means to call out His messengers so as to fulfill His promise of redemption. It certainly does not prove God effectually regenerates some who hear their message by secret, inward, irresistible means so as to ensure their willing response.

Is there not uniqueness to the call of God's chosen apostles from Israel? What set Paul and the other apostles apart as authoritative messengers of God? Paul explains in Eph. 3:1–13 that the mystery revealed to him was that Gentiles are included in Israel's promises through faith in Christ. Many other passages could be cited to demonstrate the apostle's calling and each of them should be studied carefully in order to recognize what sets apart these uniquely chosen Israelite messengers from those who come to believe through their message.[134] An egotistic, Western mindset might be more likely to presume that all believers are chosen and called out in the same manner as the apostles. We must be careful not to take this self-centered approach to interpretation.

We have observed that God judicially hardens the calloused Israelites so as to accomplish redemption. We have also seen that God uses persuasive means, like signs and wonders, to call out some from Israel to fulfill the purpose for which this nation was elected. This purpose included (1) setting apart certain Israelites to be the lineage of the Messiah, and (2) setting apart certain Israelites to carry His divinely-inspired message to the world (by use of externally persuasive

---

[134] Rom. 1:1; 11:13; 15:15–17; 16:25–26; Acts 9:15; 15:11–12; 20:24; 26:16; 1 Cor. 1:1, 17; 3:10; 4:16; 9:17; 11:1, 23; 14:37; 15:3–4, 8; 2 Cor. 1:1; Gal. 1:1, 6–9, 11–12, 15; 2:2; Eph. 1:1; Phil. 3:17; 4:9; Col. 1:1, 26–29; 1 Tim. 1:1, 11, 16; 2 Tim. 1:1, 11; 2:8; Tit. 1:1–3; 2 Pet. 3:15–16.

means), and (3) temporarily blinding the rest of Israel to accomplish redemption through their rebellion.

However, there is no indication in Scripture that (1) all those who believed the appointed messenger's teachings were likewise set apart by such persuasive means (especially not inward effectual means), or (2) that all those who did not believe the appointed messenger's teachings were likewise hardened (blinded from birth) for their entire lifetime.

Some Calvinists erroneously attempt to equate salvation with the calling out of the divinely-inspired messengers, which conflates the expressed purposes of God in Israel's election.[135] Likewise, the Calvinistic interpretation convolutes mankind's natural condition from birth with Israel's judicially-hardened condition, which confuses the biblical teaching of man's ability to respond to the gospel.[136]

The fulfillment of God's Word has never depended on the faithfulness of the Israelite people (Rom. 3:1-7). The Potter will accomplish His plan and bring to pass the promise He first made to Abraham even when His elect nation is unfaithful.

Notice that this is still a part of the apostle's response to the question first raised in Romans 9:1-6. *If God has entrusted His Word to the Israelites (vv. 4–5) and the Israelites are standing in opposition to His Word (vv. 2–3), then has God's Word failed (vs. 6)?* Not only has God not failed to fulfill His Word, but He has fulfilled it through both the active hardening and "mercying" of Israelites to the benefit of all the nations

---

[135] "Jesus' choosing of the twelve apostles (John 15:16) is almost an exact parallel, as is the choosing of Pharaoh (Rom. 9:17-18). The fact that God used Pharaoh for His redemptive purposes did not require the latter to be saved, and the same is true of Israel. If God wants to use the Jews in His service yet deny them salvation because of their unbelief, that is perfectly consistent with His righteous nature and His covenant promises. God is completely within His rights when He does this (Rom. 9:19-21)." Cottrell, 6.

[136] Piper, *Justification*, 49.

of the earth, as was the original promise made to Abraham. The apostle once again turns to Scripture to make his case.

Romans 9:25–26

As he says in Hosea: "I will call them my people who are not my people; and I will call her my loved one who is not my loved one," and, "In the very place where it was said to them, You are not my people, there they will be called children of the living God."

The apostle quotes from the prophet Hosea, which reads,

> "'In that day I will respond,' declares the Lord—'I will respond to the skies, and they will respond to the earth; and the earth will respond to the grain, the new wine and the olive oil, and they will respond to Jezreel. I will plant her for myself in the land; I will show my love to the one I called Not my loved one. I will say to those called Not my people, 'You are my people; and they will say, You are my God.'

> The Lord said to me, 'Go, show your love to your wife again, though she is loved by another man and is an adulteress. Love her *as the Lord loves the Israelites, though they turn to other gods* and love the sacred raisin cakes.'" (Hos. 2:21–3:1, emphasis added)

In the original context the author acknowledges God's genuine love for Israel despite her rebellion.

This echoes the repeated sentiment of Paul. [137] God has not given up on the Israelites, not even the ones who have turned to other gods. However, by their rebellion God has grafted in a people who historically have not been known to be His people (Rom. 11:12, 19). And they are grafted in by faith, not by unconditional, effectual means.

The Gentiles are introduced in vs. 24, in relation to their benefitting from the redemptive plan God has brought to pass through both the noble and ignoble vessels formed by the merciful Potter from the unfaithful lump of Israelite clay. Paul is using the Scriptures to demonstrate that this has always been God's mysterious redemptive plan (Eph. 3:1-13).

Rom. 9:27–33
Isaiah cries out concerning Israel: "Though the number of the Israelites be like the sand by the sea, only the remnant will be saved. For the Lord will carry out His sentence on earth with speed and finality. It is just as Isaiah said previously: "Unless the Lord Almighty had left us descendants, we would have become like Sodom, we would have been like Gomorrah."

What then shall we say? That the Gentiles, who did not pursue righteousness, have obtained it, a righteousness that is by faith; but the people of Israel, who pursued the law as the way of righteousness, have not attained their goal. Why not? Because they pursued it not by faith but as if

---

[137] F. F. Bruce, 184-185.

**it were by works. They stumbled over the
stumbling stone. As it is written:**

**"See, I lay in Zion a stone that causes peo-
ple to stumble and a rock that makes them
fall, and the one who believes in Him will
never be put to shame."**

The closing words of Romans 9 serve as an inspired commentary on the overall intention of Paul
throughout this passage. The apostle turns to Isa.
10:22–23 to show that though the number of natural
descendants are as countless as all the sand of the sea,
only those Israelites who, like the Gentiles, pursue
righteousness by faith, would attain it (Rom. 9:30).
Once again, this addresses the common misconcep-
tion that being a child of Abraham guaranteed salvation (Rom. 9:7), or being outside natural Israel ex-
cluded one from salvation (Rom. 9:24).

God intended to cut off Israel and graft in the
Gentiles. The Potter has sovereignly orchestrated both
the cutting off of Israel (by way of Judicial hardening)
and the engrafting of the Gentiles (by way of the gospel
appeal) in the climactic fulfillment of His promise to
Abraham to bless all the families of the earth.[138]

Israel, having grown calloused in their rebellion
(Rom. 9:1-3; Acts 28:27), missed their own Messiah
(Rom. 9:4-5), which certainly would lead one to ask,

---

[138] "The expression apo merous ("in part") is perhaps most naturally
taken adverbially: 'A hardening has come in part on Israel.' The alternative is
to construe it as an adjectival phrase modifying 'Israel': 'A hardening has come
on Israel in part.' If we adopt the adverbial interpretation, it seems most reasonable to conclude that the partial hardening pertains to Jewish response to
the Christian gospel about Jesus, not to a general blindness toward righteousness and the meaning of the Scriptures... The 'hardening of Israel means not
that Israel is, on the whole, blind but that God has given Israel a limited blind
spot toward Christ." Charles H. Cosgrove, *Elusive Israel* (Louisville: Westminster John Knox Press, 1997), 16-17.

Has God's Word failed (Rom. 9:6)? But even their stumbling was used in God's sovereign and redemptive plan, as Paul proves by pointing to the prophecy in Isa. 28:16, "Behold, I lay in Zion a stone of stumbling and a rock of offense."

God tells Isaiah that Israel, with their calloused hearts, will reject Him as God's messenger (Isa. 6:9-10). Jesus (Matt. 13:14-15) and Paul (Acts 28:25-27) interpreted this as a reference to Israel's rejection of Jesus as God's Messiah. For Paul, Israel's hardening paved the way to a ministry of engrafting the Gentiles (Acts 28:28; Rom. 10-11), and was not intended by God to be final, but only until the fullness of the Gentile's engrafting was accomplished (Rom. 11:25). Given that Paul expected his own ministry to produce this provoking envy to salvation (Rom. 11:14), there is no reason to suggest he believed this fulfillment was some future eschatological prophecy.

The fellow kinsmen for whom Paul desperately pleads in Romans 9 are not without hope. Those hardened have hope of being provoked by envy and saved. Those stumbling have not stumbled beyond the hope of recovery (Rom. 11:11). Paul desperately holds out hope for those cut off to leave their unbelief and be grafted back in (Rom. 11:23). Hope does not remain for the reprobate of Calvinism, but it most certainly remains for those whom the apostle addresses in this text.

Chapter 6

The Potter's Plan

Back when I was a Calvinist serving on a church staff, I had a very bright college student dare to question my theological views. I vaguely recall him quoting something from a few early Church Fathers, men I honestly knew nothing about at the time. I quickly found a heretical label to slap on them so as to dismiss their arguments. That typically placated my mind from feeling the need to dig any deeper on those issues for which I had no reply.

I distinctly remember thinking this kid had a lot to learn about the Scriptures. He was one of the few young men I had influence over that I was unable to win over to Calvinism. I used to think somewhat low of him, because he was "not willing to submit to clear reading of the Scripture." Looking back, I now have the highest respect. He thought for himself. He questioned his teachers. He studied the scholars. He sought out truth. He listened to that restless spirit within that just would not give up searching for the God revealed by the Word.

More recently I saw this young man again, not near as young, now married with a couple of kids. We reminisced about our time together in ministry and I shared with him about my journey out of Calvinism. I ended by apologizing for not being more willing to objectively examine my own perspective and consider his views more thoroughly.

He looked like he had seen a ghost. Eyes wide open, jaw dropped. He told me that of all the Calvinists he knew he would have considered me to be the last one to ever recant my views. I asked him why he thought that and he said something interesting, "Because I could tell you really believed it, I mean you were passionate about it. You talked about the TULIP like they were your kids." I dropped my head and just apologized again. He was very gracious.

I asked him what specifically kept him from being convinced by my persuasive arguments and irresistible charm (we both laughed at that one). He said without much of a hesitation, "It was Romans 9." That piqued my interest. I asked for more detail.

He said, "When I read Romans 9 through 11 I was proud of God, because I understood Paul to mean that God was doing whatever it took to redeem His world and show mercy to all, but every time I began to consider Calvinism I felt ashamed of God, like I would have to hide this fact from my friends. It just did not set well with me. I simply could not swallow it."

His comments reminded me of all the "closet Calvinists," who kept their views secret because of its inherent offensiveness, even to believers. Notable Calvinists likewise give testimony as to how difficult these doctrines are to accept when first confronted with them. Calvin himself even refers to these teachings as a "dreadful decree."[139]

This interaction reminded me of another story from early in my ministry as a young student pastor. I counseled with a middle-aged couple that had a rebellious twenty-year-old son still living at home. He would stay out all hours, come home drunk or high, and wreak havoc in their family. The poor couple was

---

[139] John Calvin wrote, "Again I ask: whence does it happen that Adam's fall irremediably involved so many peoples, together with their infant offspring, in eternal death unless because it so pleased God? Here their tongues, otherwise so loquacious, must become mute. The decree is dreadful indeed, I confess." ("Decretum quidem horribile, fateor." VG: "Je confesse que ce decret nous doit epouvanter.") Yet no one can deny that God foreknew what end man was to have before He created him, and consequently foreknew because He so ordained by His decree." John Calvin, Institutes, III.xxiii.7, (Ford Lewis Battles translation), 955-956.

a wreck and seeking godly counsel. We talked for a while about the root of the issue, but I finally ended up directing them to Paul's teaching in 1 Corinthians chapter 5 where the church had to deal with a brother living in perpetual rebellion. Paul advised the church to cast the brother out "so that his spirit may be saved in the day of the Lord Jesus" (vs. 5).

I carefully explained to this heartbroken couple that sometimes the most loving thing a parent can do for a wayward child is to let them go (Lk. 15:11-32). Even non-Christian counselors have modeled the advice of Scripture by "refusing to enable someone in their addictions."[140] This is painful and incredibly difficult to do to someone you genuinely love.

The hurting couple followed this biblical counsel and ended up having to kick their own beloved son out of their home. When other church members would ask the couple about him, they would become incredibly uncomfortable and often change the subject as quickly as possible. One day I asked his mother why she always diverted attention away from what had happened. She told me she was ashamed of what they had done. She believed it was really the best thing for them to do, but she did not believe others would see it that way. She thought others would think she was a terrible mother for kicking her own son out of their home.

It took months for her to realize she had nothing for which to be ashamed because what she had done was purely from the heart of love and a genuine desire for reconciliation with her child. Last I heard, their son had finally hit rock bottom and was in a rehab facility hoping for a full recovery.

What in the world does that story have to do with Romans 9-11 and the natural tendency of some to feel

---

[140] Reference to: Bradford Health Service, "4 Steps to Take When Someone Refuses Treatment." Quote taken from: https://bradfordhealth.com/4-steps-take-someone-refuses-treatment; [date accessed: 4/4/15].

ashamed about what it appears to teach? The feeling of shame comes from the belief that God has cut off large portions of humanity for some nefarious or self-seeking reason. Some skip these texts or hide them in closets because they read of a heavenly Father who has kicked out much of His own creation, and it is a bit embarrassing. It's hard to swallow. It's controversial.

But, should it be embarrassing? Should we be any more embarrassed about what God is doing in Romans 9-11 than what that couple did to their wayward son? Now, as a non-Calvinistic believer, I can unashamedly answer that question, "Absolutely not!"

God was acting solely out of a heart of mercy and a genuine desire for the reconciliation of every individual (Luke 19:42). He is cutting off Israelites not because He hated them from before the creation of the world. He is cutting them off in mercy, like the heartbroken couple longing to bring their son to repentance and reconciliation by locking him out of their home. Our heavenly Father is longing for the repentance of every calloused Israelite. In His divine wisdom, He knows that is best accomplished through cutting them off rather than enabling them in their rebellion.

Right now stop and re-read Romans 9 through 11 all the way through from start to finish with this merciful motive in mind. See if you find a divine Father shamefully cutting off children before they are even born, or see if you find a Father mercifully seeking and even longing for the reconciliation of all. See if you find a Father you want to brag on from the rooftops or one who has some characteristics you would rather keep buried in a closet. See if you find a Father who has cut humanity off from birth in order to show off His wrath, or rather One willing to cut Himself off in order to show off His mercy. The Father Paul reveals is made abundantly clear in his concluding sentence:

"For God has shut up all in disobedience so that He may show mercy to all." (Rom. 11:32)

God has cut us all off in our sin by giving us the inheritance to squander as prodigals and a forbidden fruit from which to take our own rebellious bite. He has allowed us all to go our own way. Why? To show off His meticulous deterministic power by predestining most to eternal torment from before creation? By no means! That is not what Paul is shouting from his rooftop.

Paul has no reason to be ashamed of his conclusions about the Father revealed in these pages of Scripture because the motive of his Father is mercy for all. We can rest assured that the Potter's plan is to show mercy to all, because that was His original promise made to Abraham..."all the families of the earth will be blessed" (Gen. 12:3). The promise is not for a few preselected families, or some particular group elected before creation, but for every single family of the earth!

The promise of our sovereignly free Potter is inclusive, not exclusive. The Potter at the wheel in Paul's narrative is a merciful Potter; One whose calling is irrevocable (11:29) and promises sure (9:4-6). He is a Potter with a redemptive purpose, a purpose He fulfills through molding unfaithful vessels for both noble and common uses (9:21). He is a Potter who weeps over His hardened clay while longing to reconcile them from their rebellious ways (Lk. 19:42, Matt. 23:37, Rom. 10:21, 2 Cor. 5:20). He is a Potter you would want to tell your friends all about, every single detail.

Why? Because He is a good, gracious Potter who always, and I mean always, keeps His promise!

Appendix:

Answering the Calvinist's Most Popular Argument

"Why did you believe the gospel, but your friend did not? Are you wiser or smarter or more spiritual or better trained or more humble?"

This is typically one of the first questions a Calvinist will ask a non-Calvinist when attempting to convince them of their doctrine.[141] In fact, when I was a Calvinist, I used this argument more often than any other, and it was quite effective. However, I have come to believe there are at least four significant problems with this line of argumentation:

1) Question Begging Fallacy

A question begging fallacy presumes true the very point up for debate, and the question above presumes a deterministic answer is required.[142] It is tantamount

---

[141] John Piper said, "I rarely meet Christians who want to take credit for their conversion. There is something about true grace in the believer's heart that makes us want to give all the glory to God. So, for example, if I ask a believer how he will answer Jesus's question at the last judgment, 'Why did you believe on me, when you heard the gospel, but your friends didn't, when they heard it?' very few believers answer that question by saying: 'Because I was wiser or smarter or more spiritual or better trained or more humble.'" Quote taken from: http://www.desiringgod.org/articles/what-we-believe-about-the-five-points-of-calvinism#Grace; [date accessed: 4/2/15].

[142] Question begging is the logical fallacy of presuming true the very argument up for debate. By asking what determined a man's choice, the questioner is presuming someone or something other than that man made the determination, thus presuming true the foundation for deterministic logic (i.e., "a theory or doctrine that acts of the will, occurrences in nature, or social or psychological phenomena are causally determined by preceding events or natural laws [or Divine decree]." Merriam-Webster Dictionary). While a determiner may state reasons or influential factors for his or her own determination (i.e., I

to asking, "What determined the response of you and your friend?" As if something or someone other than the responsible agents themselves made the determination. The question presumes determinism is true and that libertarian free will is not possible.[143]

I believe that the cause of a choice is the chooser (or the cause of a determination is the determiner) and accept the mystery associated with the functioning of that free will in making its own determinations. Now, Calvinists will often challenge my appeal to mystery at this point as if it is a weakness unique to my libertarian worldview. This is a very shortsighted argument, however, which will be made abundantly clear in the next point.

2) Calvinists Ultimately Appeal to the Same Mystery

While the Calvinist may feel he has the "upper hand" when asking about the "decisive factor" in man's choice to reject God's Words, the role reverses quite dramatically when the conversation shifts to man's first choice to reject God's Words. Whether discussing Satan's first act of rebellion or Adam's first choice to sin, it becomes quite evident that the Calvinist has painted himself into a corner by denying libertarian free will.

---

chose to overeat because it tastes so good) that does not mean the factors listed effectually caused the determination (i.e., the taste of food determined the agent's choice to overeat). The agent alone made the determination based on the factors taken into consideration and deliberated upon. To presume without proof that something or someone outside the agent himself made the determination (i.e., was the "decisive factor") is question begging. So too, presuming that one's desires are determined by one's nature in such a manner that any given moral choice could not have been other than it was by necessity is likewise question begging.

[143] Libertarian Free Will is "the categorical ability of the will to refrain or not refrain from a given moral action."

While arguing that mankind will always act in accordance with his nature (assuming the nature could not be libertarianly free, mind you), the Calvinist has no rational answer as to why Adam (or Lucifer) chose to rebel.[144] For instance, John Piper openly admits:

"How God freely hardens and yet preserves human accountability we are not explicitly told. It is the same mystery as how the first sin entered the universe. How does a sinful disposition arise in a good heart? The Bible does not tell us."[145]

And R.C. Sproul similarly teaches,

"But Adam and Eve were not created fallen. They had no sin nature. They were good creatures with a free will. Yet they chose to sin. Why? I don't know. Nor have I found anyone yet who does know."[146]

As you can clearly see, the Calvinist has just "kicked the can down the road," so to speak, when it comes to appealing to the mystery of free moral will. They eventually appeal to the same mystery that we do, all the while thinking they are taking the higher

---

[144] On the one hand, Calvinists argue that mankind always chooses according to their greatest inclination which is ultimately determined by their God-given nature, yet on the other hand they affirm that Adam "was perfectly free from any corruptions or sinful inclinations," and that he "had no sinful inclinations to hurry him on to sin; he did it of His own free and mere choice." Jonathan Edwards, *"All God's Methods Are Most Reasonable," in Sermons and Discourses: 1723-1729*, ed. by Kenneth P. Minkema, Works 14 (1997): 168.

How does the affirmation of Adam's freedom to sin or refrain from sin not violate the Calvinists own definition of human will and choice? For Adam to choose to sin he must violate the law of his own nature, as defined by the Calvinistic systematic.

[145] John Piper, accessed online from: http://www.desiringgod .org/sermons/the-hardening-of-pharaoh-and-the-hope-of-the-world; [date accessed: 4/2/15].

[146] RC Sproul, *Chosen By God*, p.31

moral ground by giving God all the credit for the Christian's choice to trust in Christ. In reality, however, by not accepting the mystery of man's free will, the Calvinist has created a new mystery that is simply not afforded by the text of Scripture. This problem is made evident by turning the question around and asking this of the Calvinist, "Why has your lost friend continued to hate and reject God?"

Most Calvinists do not want to admit that the reprobate of their system ultimately hates and rejects God because God first hated and rejected them. Calvinists would rather focus on the elect who are saved by deterministic means while ignoring the inevitable conclusions about the non-elect who remain damned for the same deterministic reason. This is a dilemma unique to their worldview, not a tension created by the teachings of Scripture.

So, the Calvinist rejects the mystery of libertarian freedom only to adopt another even more difficult mystery. One that arguably brings into question the holiness, righteousness and trustworthiness of our God - namely the suggestion that God is implicit in the determination of moral evil, as evidenced by John Calvin's own teachings:

> "...how foolish and frail is the support of divine justice afforded by the suggestion that evils come to be, not by His will but by His permission...It is a quite frivolous refuge to say *that God otiosely permits them, when Scripture shows Him not only willing, <u>but the author of them</u>*...Who does not tremble at these judgments with which God works in the hearts of even the wicked whatever He will, rewarding them nonetheless according to desert? Again it is quite clear from the evidence of Scripture that God works in the hearts of men to incline their wills just as he will, whether to good

for His mercy's sake, or to evil according to their merits."[147]

Which mystery is more difficult to swallow? One that seemingly suggests mankind might have some part to play in reconciliation (the bringing together of two parties) or the one that suggests God is the *author of evil* (that which divided the two parties to begin with)?[148] More importantly, which of these mysteries does the Bible actually afford?

3) Better by Choice or Divine Decree is Still Better

Why does one individual believe and the other one does not? The Traditionalist can rightly say that God created both individuals with genuine responsibility (ability-to-respond), whereas the consistent Calvinist must admit that one individual was made "better" than the other by means outside of either individual's control (i.e., irresistible grace or effectual regeneration).

Therefore, it is the Calvinist who ultimately has to admit to all the unbelievers of the world, "We chose to believe in Christ because God made us morally better people than the rest of you." Whereas the Traditionalist would say, "No, everyone has the same God-given moral capacity to believe in Christ, no one is made morally 'better' by God. If you refuse to believe there

---

[147] John Calvin, *The Eternal Predestination of God*, 10:11 [emphasis added].

[148] In contrast to Calvin's quote, many Calvinists (as reflected in their confessional statements) deny that God is "the author of evil." One must wonder, however, what distinction with an actual difference is there in God authoring evil in contrast to His "decreeing it," "bringing it about for His glory," "causally determining it," or His "meticulous providence over" it.

is no one to blame but yourself, because God gave you everything you needed."

Whether one believes because they were sovereignly made to do so or simply given the ability to do so freely does not change the fact that believers are doing something "morally better." (But, as we will discover in the next point, better does not mean "worthy of salvation.") Therefore, the Traditionalist would never say, "I am more capable of humbling myself than my unbelieving friend." But the consistent Calvinist, on the other hand, has to say, "Yes, God did irresistibly make me morally better, smarter, and more capable of humbling myself than my non-believing friend."

An unbeliever could rightly say to the Calvinist, "How arrogant of you to think that God made you humbler or smarter," whereas if they said that to the Traditionalist, we could rightly answer, "No He didn't, you have no such excuse. You have just as much moral ability to understand the gospel and humble yourself as I have. God has granted us both that moral responsibility."

Non-Calvinists are too often accused that we could or would boast in our salvation because we affirm that it is our responsibility to freely respond in faith to the gracious Holy Spirit inspired gospel appeal. But, is this really boastworthy?

We are the ones who teach that anyone can believe the gospel. Why would we boast in doing something anyone is able to do? It is uniquely the Calvinistic systematic that claims this moral ability is especially given to them and not most people. It makes much more sense for a Calvinist to boast in an ability granted to him that has been withheld from most others.

A great singer, for example, is a given a rare gift from birth and can often become proud or boastful due to that unique gift. But, if everyone was born able sing equally well, then boasting in that ability would not make any sense. Thus, Calvinism leaves more room for boasting than does our soteriological perspective.[149] This also speaks to the biblical teaching on the attainability of goodness or righteousness, which we will discuss in the next point.

4) A Decision does not Merit Salvation, even if it's a Libertarianly Free Decision

What is the underlying motivation for asking the question, "Why you and not another?" The implication seems to be that one who makes the libertarianly free decision to accept the gospel appeal is meriting salvation. As if the decision to repent somehow earns one's forgiveness. But, asking for forgiveness does not merit being forgiven, just as admitting you cannot fulfill the entire law does not fulfill the entire law.

Think of it this way: Did the prodigal son earn, merit or in any way deserve the reception of his father on the basis that he humbly returned home? Of course not. He deserved to be punished, not rewarded. The acceptance of his father was a choice of the father alone and it was ALL OF GRACE. The father did not have to forgive, restore and throw a party for his son on the basis that he chose to come home. That was the father's doing.

Humiliation and brokenness is not considered "better" or "praiseworthy" and it certainly is not inherently valuable. In fact, one could argue that it was weak and pitiful of the son to return home and beg his daddy for a job instead of working his own way out of

---

[149] To be clear, I do not believe true Christians from either soteriological system would actually boast in such things. This is merely a rebuttal to those who attempt to argue that our soteriological system would somehow promote boasting.

that pig sty. The only thing that makes this quality "desirable" is that God has chosen to grace those who humble themselves, something He is in no way obligated to do (Is. 66:2). God gives grace to the humble not because a humble response deserves salvation, but because He is gracious.

Calvinists often conflate man's choice to confess with God's choice to forgive while labeling it all "salvation." They go on to convincingly argue that God is "sovereign over salvation," which to a Calvinist actually means, God is as much in control over man's choice to repent in faith as He is over His own choice to forgive the repentant. It would be tantamount to the father being just as in control over his son's return home as he was over his gracious choice to receive him back when he got there. This is simply never established biblically.

It's difficult to argue with someone who is making the case that God is "in control of salvation" and thus is "the One who gets all credit for salvation," but that difficulty only exists due to the conflating of man's responsibility to believe/confess with God's gracious choice to save whosoever does so. Of course salvation is all of God, but that is distinct from man's responsibility to humbly trust in Him for salvation. We cannot conflate the son's choice to come home with the father's gracious choice to receive him back when he gets there.

We all affirm that salvation belongs to the Lord, but that does not mean sin and the responsibility to repent from sin also belongs to the Lord. God has given us the responsibility to repent in faith and there is no biblical reason to suggest we are not morally able to respond to God's own gracious appeals to do so. Clearly Scripture calls us to humility and there is nothing which suggests we cannot respond in humility when confronted by the powerful, clear revelation of

God's convicting, life-giving truth through the law and the gospel. Consider what our Lord taught us in Luke 18:10-14:

> "Two men went up into the temple to pray, one a Pharisee and the other a tax collector. The Pharisee stood and was praying this to himself: 'God, I thank You that I am not like other people: swindlers, unjust, adulterers, or even like this tax collector. 'I fast twice a week; I pay tithes of all that I get.' But the tax collector, standing some distance away, was even unwilling to lift up his eyes to heaven, but was beating his breast, saying, 'God, be merciful to me, the sinner!' I tell you, this man went to his house justified rather than the other; for everyone who exalts himself will be humbled, but he who humbles himself will be exalted."

Did the tax collector deserve to go home justified because of his humble admission of guilt? Of course not. If that were so, then his confession would have merited his salvation and there would be no reason for Christ's death to atone for his sin. He went home justified because of God's grace and provision alone! Maintaining man's libertarianly free responsibility to repent and believe does not negate the truth that salvation is completely and totally of God alone.

Throughout the Scriptures we see examples of God "finding favor" in believing individuals (Job, Enoch, Noah, Abram, etc), but these men, like all of humanity, still fell short of God's glory and were unrighteous according to the demands of God's law. They needed a savior. They needed redemption and reconciliation. Even those who believe the truth of God's revelation deserve eternal punishment for their sin.

What must be understood is that no one was righteous according to the demands of the law. However, that does NOT mean that all people are unable to believe God's revealed truth so as to be credited as righteous by God's grace. Paul taught that no one was righteous in Romans 3, yet he turns around and declares in the very next chapter that "Abraham believed God, and it was credited to him as righteousness" (4:3).

How can that be? Has Paul contradicted himself? First he declares that no one is righteous and then he tells us that Abraham was righteous? Which is it?

Of course Paul is not contradicting himself, he is drawing the distinction between righteousness by works (Rm. 3:10-11) and righteousness by grace through faith (Rm. 3:21-24). The former is unattainable but the latter has always been very much attainable by anyone, which again, is why all are "without excuse" (Rm. 1:20).

God can show mercy on whomever He wants to show mercy! We happen to know, based on biblical revelation, that God wants to show mercy to those who humbly repent in faith, which is man's responsibility, not God's.

Calvinists argue, "If a person becomes humble enough to submit to God it is because the Holy Spirit has given that person a new, humble nature..."[150] In other words, Calvinists believe that humility is an effectual result of regeneration. Therefore, one has to be regenerate in order to even recognize and admit their need for regeneration. But, is humility the result of an effectual work of God? If so, then clearly the opposite must also be true. Prideful sin must be the result of an

---

[150] Quote taken from Reformation Theology web site accessed online: http://www.reformationtheology.com/2006/07/ is_faith_the_gift_of_god_- what.php; [date accessed: 8/2/16].

equally effectual work of God (namely His eternal decree to seal all man over into a state of moral inability from birth due to the sin of another, which makes one morally incapable of humbling himself).

It may surprise some to hear that I do believe God effectually humbles some people. I just do not believe those people will be saved. If you wait on God to effectually humble you, it will be too late! This is one of the dangers of the Calvinistic worldview. If taken consistently it removes the responsibility that Scripture clearly places on man and puts it onto God.

Look at what Jesus taught in Matthew 23:12, "Whoever exalts himself shall be humbled; and whoever humbles himself shall be exalted." Let's consider the first phrase of Christ's teaching, *"Whoever exalts himself shall be humbled..."*

This is "effectual humility!" God will effectually humble those who exalt themselves and notice that these "effectually humbled" people will be eternally separated from God. God does not effectually humble everyone! He only effectually humbles those who refuse to humble themselves.

As Christ goes on to say, *"whoever humbles himself shall be exalted."* In other words, you must humble yourself or God will do it for you in judgment. Yet, Calvinists teach God effectually humbles everyone:

- On Calvinism God effectually humbles the elect unto salvation.
- On Calvinism God effectually humbles the non-elect unto damnation.

You must ask yourself if this was Christ's intent in this passage or any other? Is God responsible for whether or not you humbly confess your sin or is that your responsibility?

What does the Bible say about our responsibility?

1 Peter 5:5-6: "God opposes the proud but shows favor to the humble. *Humble yourselves,* therefore, under God's mighty hand, that He may lift you up in due time."

Isaiah 66:2: "These are the ones I look on with favor: those *who are humble and contrite* in spirit, and who tremble at my word."

James 4:10: "*Humble yourselves* before the Lord, and He will lift you up."

2 Kings 22:19: "Because your heart was responsive and you *humbled yourself* before the Lord when you heard what I have spoken against this place and its people—that they would become a curse and be laid waste—and because you tore your robes and wept in my presence, I also have heard you, declares the Lord."

2 Chronicles 12:7: "When the Lord saw that they humbled themselves, this word of the Lord came to Shemaiah: 'Since they have *humbled themselves,* I will not destroy them but will soon give them deliverance. My wrath will not be poured out on Jerusalem through Shishak.'"

2 Chronicles 12:12: "Because Rehoboam *humbled himself,* the Lord's anger turned from him, and He was not totally destroyed."

Zephaniah 2:3: "Seek the Lord, all you humble of the land, you who do what He commands. *Seek* *righteousness, seek humility*; perhaps you will be sheltered on the day of the Lord's anger."

Matthew 18:4: "Whoever *humbles himself* like this child is the greatest in the kingdom of heaven."

Matthew 23:12: "For those who exalt themselves will be humbled, and those who *humble themselves* will be exalted."

Luke 14:11: "For all those who exalt themselves will be humbled, and those who *humble themselves* will be exalted."

Luke 18:14: "I tell you that this man, rather than the other, went home justified before God. For all those who exalt themselves will be humbled, and those who *humble themselves* will be exalted."

As stated earlier, we cannot conflate man's responsibility to humble themselves with God's gracious choice to save the humble. God shows mercy to whomever He wants to show mercy (Rom. 9:15), but it is no secret to whom God wishes to show mercy.

Isaiah 66:2: "These are the ones I look on with favor: those who are humble and contrite in spirit, and who tremble at my word."

Psalm 18:27: "You save the humble but bring low those whose eyes are haughty."

Psalm 25:9: "He guides the humble in what is right and teaches them His way."

Psalm 147:6: "The Lord sustains the humble but casts the wicked to the ground."

Proverbs 3:34: "He mocks proud mockers but shows favor to the humble and oppressed."

Matthew 5:3: "Blessed are the poor in spirit, for theirs is the kingdom of heaven."

Luke 1:52: "He has brought down rulers from their thrones but has lifted up the humble."

James 4:6: "But He gives us more grace. That is why Scripture says: 'God opposes the proud but shows favor to the humble.'"

The only time Scripture teaches us that God effectually humbles man is in judgment. Every other time the inspired text clearly places that responsibility on us to *humble ourselves*. God shows favor to those who humble themselves in faith and it is His gracious choice alone that saves.

Should Implies Could

At this point in the conversation a Calvinist will often insist that the biblical commands to humble yourself, like the rest of the law, cannot be fulfilled by a fallen person. They will argue that apart from God's irresistible work of grace, no one would humble themselves and confess their sins. But, doesn't the command strongly imply one's ability to fulfill that command?

If I told my son to clean up his room it would strongly imply that I believed it was within his abilities to do so, especially if I punished him for failure to complete the task. No decent parent would tell their two day old infant to clean up a mess and then punish them for not doing so. Such an action would expose the parent as insane or completely immoral.

This is basic common sense, but is it applicable to how God deals with humanity? Is the implication in Scripture of "you should" mean that "you could?" I think we can all agree that "ought" strongly implies moral ability for all practical purposes, but is that a biblical reality? Sometimes the Bible defies our practical sensibilities and turns our reality up on its ear. Is that the case here? Do God's expressions of what we SHOULD do imply that we actually COULD do it?[151]

Could the "Rich Young Ruler" have willingly given up his wealth to follow Christ as Zacchaeus does in the very next chapter (Lk. 18-19)? Or was Zacchaeus granted an ability that was withheld from the Rich Young Ruler? *(Note: I'm speaking of man's moral/spiritual abilities to repent in faith, not their physical ability or mental assent, so the all too often rebuttal, "He is able but not willing," simply does not apply here.)*

Calvinists would agree with the Traditionalists that both Zacchaeus and the Rich Young Ruler SHOULD have given up everything to follow Christ, but only the Traditionalist maintains that both of them COULD have willingly done so.

Why do Calvinists insist that COULD does not imply SHOULD when it comes to the biblical revelation? Dr. Wayne Grudem, a Calvinistic scholar, explains the issue in this manner:

---

[151] Norman Geisler summarizes the problem in this way: "If I'm really not the cause of my actions, why should I take responsibility for them? Why should I take either credit or blame? After all, the extreme Calvinists believes that ought does not imply can. Responsibility does not imply the ability to respond. If this is so, why should I feel responsible? Why should I care when it's completely out of my hand one way or the other?" Norman Geisler, *Chosen but Free* (Bloomington, MN: Bethany House Publishers, 2001), 122.

"Advocates of the Arminian [non-Calvinist] position draw attention to the frequency of the free offer of the gospel in the New Testament. They would say that these invitations to people to repent and come to Christ for salvation, if bona fide, must imply the ability to respond to them. Thus, all people without exception have the ability to respond, not just those who have been sovereignly given that ability by God in a special way."[152]

Grudem, like John Hendryx of mongerism.com, rebuts this perspective by making arguments such as,

"What the Scriptures say we 'ought' to do does not necessarily imply what we 'can' do. The Ten Commandments, likewise, speak of what we ought to do but they do not imply that we have the moral ability to carry them out. The law of God was given so that we would be stripped of having any hope from ourselves. Even faith itself is a divine command that we cannot fulfill without the application of God's regenerative grace by the Holy Spirit."[153]

Are you following the Calvinistic argument? Here it is put very simply:

- God tells man they SHOULD keep all the commandments.
- Man CANNOT keep all the commandments.
- God also tells man they SHOULD humbly repent for breaking commandments.

[152] Wayne Grudem, *Systematic Theology: An Introduction to Biblical Doctrine* (Grand Rapids, MI: Zondervan, 1994), 341.

[153] John Hendryx, *What Do Arminianism and Hyper-Calvinism Share in Common?* Quote taken from: https://www.monergism.com/thethreshold/articles/onsite/HyperArmin.html; [date accessed: 4/14/16].

- Therefore man also CANNOT humbly repent for breaking commandments.[154]

If the fallacy in this argument is not obvious to you, please allow me to explain by way of analogy. Back when my kids were younger we did a family activity that our church had suggested. I stood at the top of the stairs with my three children at the bottom.

I said to them, "Here are the rules. You must get from the bottom of the stairs to the top of the stairs without touching any of the railing, the wall or even the stairs. Ready, go!"

My kids looked at me and then each other and then back at their mother. With bewilderment in their eyes, they immediately began to whine and complain saying, "Dad, that is impossible!"

I told them to stop whining and figure it out.

The youngest stood at the bottom and started trying to jump, slamming himself into the steps over and over. The more creative one of the bunch began looking for tools to help build some kind of contraption. Another set down on the floor while loudly declaring, "This is just stupid, no one can do that!"

---

[154] "Obligation Objection: Simply put, ought implies can and moral duties make no sense in compatibilism. 1 Cor. 10.13 can be cited as an example for libertarian freedom (God gives a way out of sin, yet we still sin). Prevenient grace seems to be a legitimate postulation, that is, the grace that precedes salvation that enables one to repent and turn from sin. Their example: P is 'we ought to avoid all sin,' and Q is 'we can avoid all sin' (ought implies can). However, it seems that some theologies (mainly Reformed), after the fall, P is true and Q is false (counterexample?). How about: P1, for any x, if x is a sin, then we ought to avoid doing x; Q1 For any x, if x is a sin, then we can avoid x. Here is where David Baggett and Jerry Walls (Arminians) show the Calvinist's fallacy of equivocation. Clearly, P1 and Q2 are true but to understand where P is true and Q is false one would need to equivocate 'all' for P as 'for each individual sin x, taken on its own' and for Q 'for the sum total of all sins added together.' An argument on equivocation seems to break at the seams. Thus, the principle of ought implies can perseveres and libertarian freedom is true." Quote taken from: http://sententias.org/2013/04/22/qa-19/; [date accessed: 11/13/16].

Finally, in exasperation one of the kids yelled out, "Dad, why don't you just help us?" I raised my eyebrows as if to give them a clue that they may be on the right track. The eldest caught on quickly.

"Can you help us dad?" he shouted.

I replied quietly, "No one even asked me."

"Can you carry us up the stairs?" he asked.

"I will if you ask me," I said.

And one by one, I carried each child to the top after they simply asked. Then, we sat down and talked about salvation. We talked about how it is impossible for us to get to heaven by our own efforts, but if we ask Christ for help then He will carry us. It was a great visual lesson of God's grace in contrast with man's works.

But suppose that my children's inability to get to the top the stairs also meant they were incapable of asking me for help. Imagine how this story would have played out if it was impossible for my children not only to get to the top of the stairs but equally impossible for them to recognize that inability and request help when it was offered.

This illustrates the mistake of Calvinism. Let's go back to their fallacy above as it relates to my story:

- Dad tells his kids they SHOULD get to the top of stairs.
- Kids CANNOT complete this task as requested.
- Dad also tells the kids they SHOULD ask for help.
- Therefore, the kids CANNOT ask for help.

Do you see the problem now? The whole purpose of presenting my kids with that dilemma was to help them to discover their need for help. To suggest that they cannot realize their need and ask for help on the basis that they cannot get to the top of stairs completely undermines the very purpose of the giving them that dilemma.

The purpose of the father in both instances is to get others to trust him. The law was not sent for the purpose of getting mankind to heaven. Just as the purpose of the activity was not to get the kids to the top of the staircase. The purpose was to help them to see that they have a need and that they cannot make it on their own.

Calvinists have wrongly concluded that because mankind is unable to attain righteousness by works through the law, they must also be equally unable to attain righteousness by grace through faith. In other words, they have concluded that because mankind is incapable of "making it to the top of the stairs," then they are equally incapable of "recognizing their inability and asking for help." It does not follow and it is not biblical. Paul said:

> **Rom. 9:30-32:** "What then shall we say? That the Gentiles, who did not pursue righteousness, have obtained it, a righteousness that is by faith; but the people of Israel, who pursued the law as the way of righteousness, have not attained their goal. Why not? Because they pursued it not by faith but as if it were by works."

It seems Calvinists would have us believe that because pursuit by works fails in attaining righteousness that a pursuit by faith would not even be possible. This is simply never taught in Scripture. When Calvinists are pressed on the obvious implication that SHOULD implies COULD, they appeal to the demands of the law, which is like appealing to my demands for the children to get to the top of the stairs without touching anything. I did not make that demand with the expectation of my children actually doing it, after all it is impossible. I made the demand to help them realize they could not do it without my help.

So too, God did not send the law with the expectation that we could actually fulfill its demands. That is not the purpose of the law. According the Scripture, "No one will be declared righteous in God's sight by the works of the law; rather, through the law we become conscious of our sin" (Rom. 3:20).

The law is a "tutor" who points us to our need for Christ (Gal. 3:24). The law was never sent for the purpose of being fulfilled by mankind, just as the stair-climbing activity was never intended to be completed by my kids. It was a "tutoring" lesson to teach my children that they must rely on someone else, a useless activity indeed if they are somehow incapable of coming to that realization or admitting their need for help.

If my kids are as completely incapable of understanding their need for help in getting to the top of stairs as they are in getting to top of the stairs without help, then why would I bother with the activity in the first place? Likewise, if mankind is as completely incapable of trusting in the One who fulfilled the law as they are in fulfilling the law themselves, then what is the point in sending an insufficient tutor to teach them a lesson they cannot learn? As Traditionalists, we actually believe God sent the world a sufficient tutor; the Calvinist does not.

The argument that SHOULD implies COULD remains virtually unanswered by the Calvinist who appeals to the law as their example. That is, unless they can demonstrate that it actually was God's intention for us to fulfill the law's demand in order to attain righteousness. After all, to conclude that man cannot fulfill the purpose of the law's demands begs the question, because it presumes man cannot fulfill the purpose of the law by believing in the One who fulfilled its demands.

Basic common sense tells us that if one ought to do something, he can do it. This is especially true if one is punished for his failure to do that which is expected. In 2 Thessalonians 2:10, Paul says of the unrighteous, "They perish because they did not accept the love of the truth in order to be saved." And in John 12:48, Jesus said, "There is a judge for the one who rejects me and does not accept my words; the very words I have spoken will condemn them at the last day."

Scripture never once says that we will perish because of Adam's sin. But over and over again it says that we will each be held accountable for our response to the clear the revelation of God. According to Paul, all men stand "without excuse" (Rom. 1:20), yet Calvinistic doctrine gives mankind the best excuse imaginable:

Judge: "Why did you remain in unbelief?"

Reprobate: "I was born hated and rejected by my God who sealed me in unbelief from the time I was born until the time I died due to the sin of another."

Can you think of any better excuse than that?
I cannot.

Packing Slip

PO BOX 22
CENTERVILLE, TN 37033

Ship To: Byron Loyd
2393 LAURELFIELD DR
GRAYSON, GA 30017-2880 US

Order #	56651
Date	9/21/2022
User	6309406703837
Ship Date	

Item	Description	Price	Qty	Ext. Price
PB1-DEMA- LAST	Last Days Madness: Obsession of the Modern Church - Paperback	$17.95	1	$17.95
PB1-DEMA- WARW	Wars and Rumors of Wars - Paperback	$14.95	1	$14.95

Sub Total:	$32.90
Tax:	$2.28
Shipping:	$5.00
Total:	$40.18

TO REORDER YOUR UPS DIRECT THERMAL LABELS:

1. Access our supply ordering web site at **UPS.COM**® or contact UPS at 800-877-8652.

2. Please refer to label #02774006 when ordering.

02774006   RRDR

Made in the USA
Columbia, SC
12 September 2022